LIFE
Tuneups

Stay True to the
amazing person
you are!

LIFE
Tuneups

**Your Personal Plan to Find Balance,
Discover Your Passion,
and Step into Greatness**

LOREN SLOCUM

life

Guilford, Connecticut
An imprint of The Globe Pequot Press

To buy books in quantity for corporate use
or incentives, call **(800) 962–0973**
or e-mail **premiums@GlobePequot.com.**

GPP Life is an imprint of The Globe Pequot Press.

Text design by Sheryl P. Kober
Layout by Joanna Beyer
Cover design by Jane Sheppard
Cover photo by Brittany Hanson

Library of Congress Cataloging-in-Publication Data is available on file.

ISBN 978-0-7627-5067-2

Printed in the United States of America

10 9 8 7 6 5 4 3 2 1

*To every woman, may you always celebrate
and honor the amazing woman you are.*

*To my daughter, Asher, this is for you,
to always remember the gift you are to this world.*

*To my mom, for being a constant example
of gentle strength.*

To my dad, my number one fan in heaven.

To my husband, Shore, for being my rock.

*And to my boys, Josua and Quinn,
for being my inspiration.*

Contents

Foreword

I first met Loren under circumstances near and dear to my heart, a precursor to what I would personally come to know of her kind and giving nature—a privilege I've experienced in nearly two decades of friendship and shared impact with her as a key team member of Robbins Research International.

Because of the kind act of a stranger who helped feed my family when I was eleven years old on Thanksgiving, I have been committed to giving back to individuals and families in similar ways ever since. Today what started with my feeding two families has grown into the Anthony Robbins Foundation "Basket Brigade," which delivers food and other necessities to more than two million families facing financial challenges around the world. I met Loren when she volunteered to support an early effort I had put together locally in the San Diego area in 1989, around the time when the Basket Brigade really began to take on a life of its own. I had invited the group of volunteers over for dinner after we delivered the meals, back when I lived in Del Mar, California.

Back at the house we all shared with each other what we were most thankful for. It was an opportunity for us to outwardly express gratitude, but also to share the almost indescribable elation of knowing that, even if only for a day, we made a difference in the lives of others. Though I did not know Loren beforehand, it later became clear to me that our fellowship that day ignited a special drive inside of her to continue living a life of contribution to others. She also connected very deeply that day with an employee and friend of mine named Shore . . . the man who would later become her sweetheart and husband! ;-)

Eventually, Loren would become a cherished and respected trainer and facilitator in the Robbins organization. Her name became synonymous with sincerity, compassion, caring, imagination, diligence, fun, and effectiveness—the qualities people look for in a colleague, mentor, and friend. Her boundless dedication inspired those she's touched over the years, including myself, even in the face of her raising a family and being on the road virtually year-round, all while pursuing her own dreams and passions, embodied here by the creation of *Life Tuneups*. Loren's story, experience, and insight within these pages are a testament to the constant, never-ending quest to live a life of meaning, passion, joy, and true authenticity. These attributes form the base of Loren's life and her life's work.

And while there are common components everyone must integrate within themselves as we move forward along the path of self-discovery—aspects that are universal to all regardless of gender, nationality, or creed—Loren's approach will particularly speak to those women who have asked the same questions that she has tackled in the various stages of her own personal and professional development. These challenges remain peerless to those women who wear the multi-faceted hats of mother, daughter, lover, nurturer, and career-woman; yet remain true to the irrevocable beauty, grace, heart, and spirit that is woman.

Most of all, though, Loren's example invigorates those ambitions of achievement and fulfillment we all have, sharpening that focus into practical, relatable, and effective steps to cultivate those dreams and make them into reality. By being that extraordinary example, she gives license to others to discover that extraordinary quality within themselves, realizing that 80 percent of accomplishment is simply a matter of unlocking who you really are at the core, nurturing that authenticity, and directing that essential self toward what is most precious in your life.

Life Tuneups is just that—Loren's testament to the simple yet profound tools for refueling, recharging, and connecting with your real self. A true leader, Loren's guidance reminds us of the gifts we contain within, gifts to be cultivated and shared. Even when we take into consideration today's challenges and uncertainties, imagining the life you want is no mere amenity. To believe that all things are attainable is to be the real you, an essence we are capable of living everyday under any conditions.

Foreword

To develop that inner strength is to live a life of peace and purpose; a life that is rich, beautiful, and meaningful no matter what may be happening on the outside.

After nineteen years of tireless devotion to growth and contribution, Loren understands and appreciates the game of life at a higher level. *Life Tuneups* represents her testimony that shifting your inner world changes your outer world, changes your life, and the lives of everyone you touch. Unlock the life that you really want for yourself. Tune up and be what you were meant to be.

—*Anthony Robbins*
December 1, 2008

True *adj:*

1. Real, genuine, authentic
2. Not deceitful
3. Such as it should be
4. Unfailing or sure

Or we could look at this another way— ***true*** *is your heart's yearning, a sense of knowing what you are here to do and what makes you feel alive and authentic.*

How Do You Tune In . . . to Your *True* Self?

Do you ever have *those* days when things seem to be going a little too fast, and you need everything to just go away, even just for a moment? So you escape to your car, close the door, and just kick back, sink into your seat, and take a big deep breath—yes, it's me time. Then you lean over and start searching for that radio station, for the one song that will allow you to just . . . be. Then you get static, static, and more static until you finally stumble across a station; it may not be the one you were originally looking for, but you find yourself listening because it is just "too hard" to *tune in* to the station you really love. Too much work, too much to even think about, as you had already been going full speed all day long!

But after a while you realize, *This is not it; this is not how I want to feel.*

Then you decide to take the time to tune in and find that station you truly love. And once you eventually hear that song, the one that reminds you who you are and what you love, what happens? Traffic—and life—stop, because you have found what really makes you feel good and brings you back to you. You find yourself moving in your seat, and finally you start to feel alive again.

Life Tuneups is *that* opportunity to tune in to *your* station! You can complain about the station you're on, or you can take the time to search for the one you really want. This is a choice you get to make. If you do decide to tune in, know that it will take a little bit of time. But once you rediscover your station, almost nothing can take away the feeling it brings.

Through stories, exercises, and examples, *Life Tune-ups* will show you how to tune in to that perfect station so that you can recharge, have the courage to reach beyond your comfort zone, and connect with your true self. This is the time to step into your greatness and leave behind any old definitions of who you are. This is your opportunity to share your gifts and make an impact not only on yourself but also on your children, your friends, and your community.

Are you ready to tune in?

How I Learned to Tune In to My Dreams

My journey back to my true self began with a lunch box. Growing up in a small town in North Carolina,

Introduction

I was quiet and shy (trust me—I've made up for lost time!). I stood out for two reasons: for being the lone Jewish girl at a Catholic school and for the trendy fashions my mom would bring back from New York for me to wear and to sell in her store. There were a few girls who would even tear and cut up my clothes as we dressed in the locker room. I tried to keep the peace and so chose not to say anything. (Have you ever done that—kept quiet because you didn't want to make it about *you*?) Meanwhile, my older brother was also being bullied—that is until I decided to stop being quiet.

One day I saw the same bullies picking on my brother, calling him names. This time, instead of remaining quiet, I decided to take a stand. I grabbed my yellow school bus lunch box, pushed the biggest guy in the group against the wall, and smacked him across the face with the lunch box, breaking his nose.

Though I was taken to the principal's office, I finally felt like I had done the right thing, and I knew that my whole world had changed in that moment. Though I would never want to hurt another person, I was sick and tired of people being mean to those who couldn't stick up for themselves. That's when I thought, *no more*— no longer would I not speak up or act for something I believed in.

From then on, friends called me "Mighty Mouse"— here she comes to save the day—and throughout my life

Introduction

I was known to always stand up for the underdog. To this day I am grateful for my commitment, faith, and conviction to doing the right thing, always, regardless of what people think.

Fast-forward a few years: I graduated from college with a bachelor of arts in journalism, and everyone expected me to move to Atlanta, go to work at CNN, and be a broadcast journalist. But then I listened to all my friends talk about traveling abroad, learning new languages, and meeting interesting people, and I started to think, *Why have you rushed to get out of school and start the job you think you have to have?*

I realized that it was time for me to do something that everyone didn't expect me to do. Of course my parents were freaked out when I told them I was moving to Vail, Colorado, to work on my doctorate of waitressing! But I had to stay true to myself. Sure I was only twenty-one years old, but it was like tuning in to that radio station; I could hear the life everyone wanted for me loud and clear (and I do mean LOUD and CLEAR), and the louder it grew, the more I needed to tune in to what *I* wanted.

So I packed up my car with garbage bags full of clothes, some snacks for the road, and a full-out passion to go explore and discover myself (get ready—we're going to talk about your discovery process very soon). I persuaded a few of my friends to take a semester off and head west to play with me. Now I had a whole herd of parents mad at me for "taking their kids out of college!"

But we played, and we played hard! Sometimes I wasn't so true to myself. And you know what? At those times, I *knew* I wasn't, but I did it anyway. Remember those times? The times when you did what was convenient instead of what your heart really wanted to do? I had times when I was so caught up in myself that I didn't think about the consequences. Once I spent the night with a guy I barely knew, and a friend lovingly reprimanded me and offered: *"You need to think to yourself that you are someone special and not just anyone can have you."* From then on I began to think about who I was, who I wasn't, and who I must become to bring a great man and stronger purpose into my life.

My trip to Vail was about expanding new territory— it was about not having to *do* anything but just enjoy life for a while. I immersed myself in my "Discovery Process." I literally gave myself time to figure out what I loved. Before I had felt as if I was always rushing to get the next thing done, to mark it off on my checklist without really taking in what I was doing. I finally started to *tune in* to myself again.

Finding My True Self
After Vail I headed to California to pursue a career in sports marketing. I thought this was going to be *it*. But

the more I spent time with the in crowd and who I was supposed to be hanging out with, the lonelier I became. Have you ever taken a good look at the people you surround yourself with and wondered, *Are they pulling me up, or are they taking me down?* I got comfortable; I was making good money and hanging out with people who were fun and convenient. But something was missing—I was missing. I had to find myself.

The tricky part is this: How do you know when you have found yourself? How do you know that's even you and not somebody else? I found myself asking: *Who do I need to become in order to create the life that truly leaves a legacy? What kind of people do I need to surround myself with? How do I need to begin each of my days and end each of my nights?* And you know what? It was scary, but I had to get to the true me.

Parents ask their kids *what* they want to be when they grow up instead of *who* they want to be. And why do we always have to wait until they grow up? Why not instill some of these values now, when they are still young? But, of course, it's never too late to get started.

I realized that I was missing the part of my life that got me up early and kept me up late: contribution—giving back to my world. (As you will see throughout this book, this is a big passion of mine!)

The Turning Point

During this time of questioning myself, my friend Tom gave me a real gift when he asked me to join him and some friends who were delivering food to the homeless on Thanksgiving. This is when I realized the part of me that had been dormant for several years—the part of me that yearned to *give back*. On Thanksgiving I arrived at a castle in Del Mar, California, with about twenty-four other people who were assembling huge baskets. I headed out with my friend to the families we were assigned. It was amazing to be the delivery person. It was truly one of the best days of my life, because I felt so alive! I loved the feeling of being with people committed to making a difference in their community. I felt like something was pulling me in the right direction for the first time in a long time.

After our deliveries I wandered around the castle, looking at the photos on the walls, and I kept noticing this one guy in pictures with presidents, celebrities, and professional athletes. Tony Robbins, the man in all of the photographs, invited me to stay for dinner with some others. After dinner Tony had us stand up and talk about what we were most grateful for. I realized that I hadn't asked myself that question in a very long time. I was so caught up in my life that I failed to take note of what I was really thankful for.

Touched by the people surrounding me that day, I felt a sense of being alive, of being present. I wasn't worried about how I was going to pay the bills or the next group I would be taking care of; I just felt in it, at home with myself.

All of these experiences led me to realize that I deserved more in my life and that I needed to make some drastic changes if I was going to be true to myself. So I gave notice to my three jobs, gave up my room at the beach, and took a round-trip of discovery. I had no idea what was next, but I knew I had to leave this chapter behind and reconnect with my true self.

I volunteered and was then hired on by Robbins Research International (RRI). I worked in the production department, planning events and overseeing volunteers. I was literally on the road 250 days a year for almost twelve years. During this time, I married my husband, Shore, and a new chapter began in which I decided to tune into what I was feeling, what I wanted— what I stood up for so many years ago as a twelve-year-old girl.

My Experience in Personal Development

So what do I have to share with you that you haven't already heard from a friend, a spouse, or your parents? Maybe some of the stories shared here will get you to explore your own story, where you have been, and what you are here to do. There is a reason you picked up this book! Now is the time to rediscover who you are at your core, and I would love to help.

For the last two decades, I have worked in the world of personal development as a trainer and facilitator for Anthony Robbins. I have also led seminars around the world for women and have coached everyone from top executives to everyday moms and dads. What does *personal development* mean? A lot of times people think it's just a pump-up, but it's more than that. It's an opportunity to reinvest in yourself and better who you are, and it's ongoing. This is what *Life Tuneups* is about—that opportunity to find the more balanced, passionate, alive you, and to step into your greatness.

I can't promise you that after you read this book, your life is going to be all better. But I can promise you this: If you implement these exercises, and really take the stories within to heart, you will feel a difference. And when challenges come (physical or mental), you will be able to handle them with much more ease and finesse.

I would love to be your coach on this journey of discovery. Sometimes I'll push you—one of the things I always tell my event participants is that I will kick you in the butt, and love you at the same time. My intention is to serve you, to make sure you feel like you got something out of this, for not only yourself, but also for a friend, a family member, or your own daughter ten years from now.

One last thing: Major changes can feel overwhelming, so let's just think of this as a little life tuneup. We don't need a whole life makeover—we just need a few shifts that will ultimately take us to an extremely fulfilling life no matter what is happening.

Let's get started!

Woman *n:*

1. The female human being
2. Having female anatomy and ability to give birth

Huh? Yuck! What is that about? A **woman** *is a nurturing spirit of limitless love and intuition; she is able to transform and adapt to anything in life. Creative, dedicated, and always resourceful, her care and commitment to something greater than herself are unsurpassed!*

CHAPTER 1

Being True to the Woman You Are

Now that we've realized the importance of tuning into who we really are, how the heck do we do it? Sometimes it's easy to lose sight of our unique essence when we are bombarded by contradictions of how we *should* be. We need to be skinny and successful—but not too successful. We need to be friendly and sexy—but not provocative. We need to be attractive, but not too pretty.

The truth is you don't have to let society define who you are. Do me a favor and try a little experiment: For the next week put away all your gossip magazines—all of 'em! For seven days stop comparing yourself to anyone else and decide to live by your own rules of how you should look, act, and be. What I hope you will see: *We* define who we are, not anyone else, unless we let them!

The foundation of our roles as women depends on how we view ourselves from the inside out. Take a diamond for example. Your different roles (mom, girlfriend, daughter, businesswoman) are like different facets of a diamond. What gives your diamond that brilliance, that special shine, is the depth of the base. The clarity and strength of that base determine and define who you really are. I say I'm a mom, a wife, a businesswoman, and a speaker, but how I show up in each of these roles is based on how I view myself as a woman and the clarity I have about who I am.

You may want to consider purchasing a journal or notebook to use as a workbook for the various self-assessment exercises throughout this book. (Check out www.lobella.com for more journal options.)

Sometimes it can be too easy to allow one role to dominate and allow the base of our diamonds to get murky. At one of my seminars I met Ellen, a thirty-seven-year-old woman who talked about her business—and only her business. She was so caught up in the significance of talking about her companies that she failed to see how disconnected she was from everyone! Our hearts hurt to watch her.

Finally on the second day, an Australian woman came up beside her and said: "Tell me about you."

Then Ellen started to cry. "All I know is my business," she said.

The other woman gently pressed her: "Is that *really* all you know?" Then the other participants began to point out all of the amazing things about Ellen—her beautiful smile, her passion, things she didn't think to

"I Am" Exercise

Grab your journal and write "I am" at least ten times down the left-hand side of the page. Then (without thinking) just start writing who you are. Here are some of my examples:

I am playful.
I am visionary.
I am magical.
I am hilarious.
I am sincere.
I am grateful.
I am creative.

Even if you feel like you're not all of these things at this exact moment, put yourself in a place of owning it 100 percent, because you have it in you!

How do you feel now that you've defined who you really are? You can't just do this once—make it a daily habit, a ritual. I do this every morning while brushing my teeth to get me ready to take on the day. How can you incorporate this simple exercise into your life?

honor about herself. From then on a new person emerged who wasn't afraid to be in the moment and explore who she was without any kind of agenda. She began to listen to herself and allow the depth of her brilliance to come out once again. She no longer allowed just one role (as businesswoman) to define her.

How many of you can identify with Ellen? Or maybe you know a friend or loved one who is using work or something else to hide her true self? We all may have caught ourselves there at one time or another and lost the truth of who we are as women, as Ellen did.

You *Can* Have It All!

So what are our roles as women? We've all been told that we can't have it all, that something has to give. Who told us that? And why is our sense of self-worth and happiness always the first thing we give away? Be you, the real you! Personally, I'm a jeans, funky shirt, and boots girl—that's who I am, and I embrace that now. Not everyone does, but I feel great that I am being the real *me*, and it shows up in how I *show up*.

I love a Bill Cosby quote I once read on a wall at a little cafe in Winter Park, Colorado: "I DON'T KNOW THE DEFINITION OF SUCCESS, BUT I KNOW FAILURE IS TRYING TO MAKE EVERYONE HAPPY ALL THE TIME." I'm here to tell you: Any woman can have a successful career, a happy home life, a great relationship, well-adjusted children, and a deep sense of inner peace and joy if she works at it. Total (and stress-free!) fulfillment

MISSING: THE DEFINITION OF A WOMAN
Can't seem to figure out who I am . . .
Can you help?

Magazines tell me that I'm supposed to look hot
while I clean the toilet, but articles tell me that my
husband can chip in, too?

The definition of a woman: Will respond to every
demand
With grace and without complaint.
Needs to have a clear list of responsibilities
And hopefully a good vacation plan.

is possible, but it takes time and a little creativity.
And every woman's version will look a little different
(thank goodness!).

Now, some of you might be saying, "Well, Loren, you
don't know about *my* life or what *I am* going through"—
and you're right. But here is what I know to be true after
working with thousands of women over the last twenty
(eek) years: Every woman can "have it all" when she
learns to stay true to who she is at her very core and
makes the game of life a winnable proposition.

Women can reclaim their inner lives and the dreams
they once had for themselves. *After all, they were never*

lost in the first place; we just have to tune back in. When you access the joy and wisdom from within yourself, you *can* have more love, joy, and laughter to give to yourself as well as to your family, friends, career, and community.

While each of us is totally unique, we are also fundamentally alike in certain ways and all too often similarly out of touch with our best, most beautiful, authentic selves. As we experience life's various stages, it's too easy to get caught up in roles, to compromise, and to fulfill others' expectations, forgetting our own. All the while, we deprive ourselves of something more, telling ourselves that we can nibble on what's left after we have taken care of everyone else.

Starving Ourselves to Exhaustion
I remember someone once offering the following example: Where's the first place the heart delivers blood to? Most people say the stomach, or the liver, or the brain. The answer is itself; the heart delivers blood to itself first. So many times we give so much to everyone else that we have nothing to give back to ourselves. How can you embrace life and feel fulfilled when you're not giving back to yourself?

As a consequence of putting everyone else first, some women reach a point where they feel stressed, empty, confused, numb, even desperate for answers. But instead of trying so hard to bury these feelings, women need to rediscover—or in some cases discover for the first time—who they are at their very core, getting back in touch with what matters most to them. That's what *Life Tuneups* is about.

But the thing is, everyone gets lost at some point in her life. You have to understand that you're not alone. Even I've been through it.

People often ask me how I manage my crazy life as a wife, mother, business owner, coach, friend, and volunteer with a schedule filled with innumerable projects and nearly constant travel. In fact, it exhausts me just to say all the things I do. But trust me: I've had times when I have lost sight of my own needs and played the role of a martyr (how many of you can relate?).

One night when I was eight months pregnant with my first son, Josua, I was in Hawaii leading a team of volunteers and organizing many logistical activities for a nine-day seminar. It had been a long event; most days began at 7:30 a.m. (with a volunteer meeting that I lead) and ended around 1:00 a.m. Back then I felt I *had* to be there every minute of every second—there was no time to rest, because I had work to do and only I could do it right! Then after nine days of grueling hours and many miles of walking the "walkalota" hotel, it was 1:30 a.m. and we had to load out right after the end of the event, as another group was moving in the next day. I had organized everyone into different rooms to break down, and then at 3:30 a.m. we were scheduled to meet in the supply room.

My feet were swelling out of my shoes like a cracked-open can of instant biscuits, and I was bone tired. At around 3:15 a.m., I crawled under a 6-foot-long table, used a giveaway shirt as a pillow and the skirting from the table as a blanket, and began to give more directives. At 3:25 a.m., I popped out from underneath the table, looked at my team, and said, "I am so sorry. I owe you all an apology. I have not served you as a leader. What kind of leader have I been by not taking care of myself or my baby? That is not leadership. I am going to bed, and if you feel the way I do, please do the same."

That was another defining moment for me. I realized right then and there, thirteen years ago, that I had to fill myself up first if I expected to be good for anyone else, and I needed to recognize when others needed to take care of themselves and give them the same opportunity. I had been running on empty, expecting to feel full, but I wasn't. And even though I was great at pretending all was fine, it wasn't, and I did *not* want to be a warning for my child—I wanted to be a great example for him.

When I was under the table, I thought about how I would want my son to see me. Would I want him to see me as a martyr or as a leader? Now, every day, I have certain things that I will stand for no matter what:

- To always stay true to myself
- To be authentic to the core
- To be the real deal

- To help those who want to be helped
- To remember that my health is my wealth
- To be grateful for my family and friends
- To remember that life is a gift
- To do it with care, do it with love
- To have no regrets at the end of each day

QUICK TUNEUP

Grab your journal and start writing what you will stand for. It doesn't have to be a long list. Even if it's just two things (you can add more later as you continue with your tuneups), but make sure they are things you are committed to doing.

The old me—the woman who was burned out (even doing something I loved!) from working too hard and trying to do everything herself—wouldn't recognize the new me. I finally started taking the time to get whole and complete, rediscovering what truly made me happy. I also set parameters around what I would and would not do so that I could create that balance. And I found that I felt refreshed and recharged. Now I'm on a mission to help you do the same.

I hope this book will inspire you, make you think, make you laugh, and most important, lead you to become the person you know you are and help you understand that you can have it all—but first you must be the person you know you are.

She's there—I promise. Let's find her.

Where the heck am I, anyway?
How can I start the journey of rediscovering when I don't know where I am to begin with?

Define Your Unique and Divine Authentic Core

To begin to find out who you are, I have three questions you need to answer honestly. There are no right or wrong answers, only answers that ring true for you. But no cheating, okay?

To begin, pull out a sheet of paper or your journal and write down your name and today's date. When you have made it through all the questions and worksheets, you can go back to this point and see how well you have progressed. We're going to begin with three questions to find your authentic self.

Now let's get to those questions. Drop all of your titles—mother, sister, wife, employer, volunteer, businesswoman—and focus on you. Let's really find what feels true to you. Everyone else can wait until you are done.

Question #1

If you had to describe who you are right here, right now as you read this, who would you say you are and what do you stand for?

I know this question is really deep and a bit scary, but it can also be fun and exciting! Recently I asked this question at an event. A very conservative, professional-looking woman named Michele raised her hand; she answered the question by describing only her roles. Then I asked her to stand up and tell me her favorite song. That was easy for her: Nickelback's "Rockstar." We all looked at her in surprise. I asked the A/V tech to play the song and then asked Michele to stand up and use adjectives, not nouns, to describe herself. For two minutes she kept telling us who she was . . . *loving, passionate, silly, intense, playful, sexy,* and on and on she went. When I asked Michele what she stood for, she again rattled off adjectives like *just, peaceful, loving, creative.* At the end of the five minutes, she didn't even look like the same person. It was like we gave her permission to let the real Michele out, and she had her own little tuneup right before our eyes!

So now it's your turn: What words—adjectives—describe you, and what do you stand for?

Question #2
Who are you committed to being after reading this book? Where are you now? Where do you want to be one year from now?

For example: I am committed to having a better understanding of what makes me tick and making a plan to move forward with my life.

Question #3
If you could have two things happen that would make you feel your life was truly better after reading this book, what would they be and why?

I hope that after reflecting on these questions you begin to really think again. I hope you begin to dream, to believe that all things are attainable, and that you can be the real you again, not just on a good day, but every day.

Take a peek at the life you really want for yourself, even if it's something you only dream about after everyone else has received your time and energy. Give yourself the chance to dream big.

A Treasure Map for Finding Yourself

Another tool that can help you dig into who you really are is a treasure map (or vision board). I learned early in

Chanelle: FINDING YOUR AUTHENTIC SELF FROM CHILDHOOD

When she looks back at her childhood—who she was, how she spent her days, what made her happy and excited—Chanelle finds she is able to get in touch with her true authentic self. As a little girl she wore a dress with spandex underneath so that she could climb trees when her parents weren't looking; she always wanted to jump off of things. She rummaged through other people's trash for wood and supplies so that she could build ramps and rails to skateboard on.

Chanelle was always outside playing sports, or settling fights on the playground. She wanted to be the best in anything she did, and she loved to learn. She ran track and played soccer, field hockey, basketball, and flag football with the boys, and she loved to ride bikes, rock climb, skateboard, wakeboard, and snow ski.

Now twenty-three years young, Chanelle is a professional snowboarder, and she has broken about twelve bones in the process of life; it's been quite a journey! At times in her life she was restricted from playing the sports she loved most and was forced to watch and reflect from the sidelines. In those times she really grew up fast.

Now when she looks back at her childhood, Chanelle sees her true self. She realizes that it was a time in her life when she felt no judgment, no expectations, no fear, and no recognition for the "outside" world. She was inspired only by her own world, her dream, her moment; she was flowing through life and doing the things she wanted to do, because it made her feel good.

Chanelle believes she became a woman when she realized that the mentality of a child is the ultimate key to happiness. We only get one life . . . why not play full-out and enjoy the whole process?

Dance with your challenges, laugh with your fears. Don't wait to feel good! You deserve it NOW! Think back to your own childhood, back when you owned who you were, without a care in the world. Can that little girl help you to get back in touch with your authentic self?

my life that you have to see it to believe it. When I was in junior high, I would cut out words and pictures from magazines and put them on my three-ring binder. I chose images and phrases that reminded me of what I wanted to feel and experience. In turn I started to notice that I did experience those things. Now I use these collections of inspiring pictures and words, or treasure maps, to keep me on track when things don't look as if they're headed in a positive direction.

I have treasure maps all over my house—one in my shower, another in my closet, and some in my planners, on my phone, and on my computer screen—they are a driving force to jump-start my day. I have my kids making them, too.

But what's the purpose of doing this? It helps me stay connected to who I am and what I have on my plate of dreams. When I'm surrounded by constant reminders of who I am, it encourages me to remain focused on being true to myself and to what I want to do with my life. Let's not make it an option to allow the everyday things—stress, responsibilities, life—to distract us from ourselves.

By keeping treasure maps all around me, I am able to regularly examine what I have on them—photos of myself, my family, and objects that remind me of who I am, my goals in life, and the mission I am here to serve. Part of tuning in to who you are and what you want lies in understanding who you have to become in order to attract the right things into your life. I know that I'm committed to being feminine, bold, honest, giving, healthy, passionate, playful, and helpful. I also want to have an impact in this world, and my treasure maps are full of images that speak to these attributes. Here I am, thirty-one years later, still using these treasure maps and getting everyone else involved (my kids, my mom, my husband, our assistant, our neighbors).

I've included words on my treasure maps that inspire me and help me when I need a moment of "Oh yeah, that's who I am." The rest of the world doesn't even have to know that I have these maps around, because they're only for me.

You can add anything you like to your treasure maps, as long as they are things that matter to you. I've found that photos and words work well for me, but you might want to draw your treasure maps or perhaps type out some of your own personal dreams to put on them.

Sit down, put on your favorite music, and grab as many magazines as you can. Start tearing out any photos, words, or phrases that catch your attention. You may not immediately understand why they speak to you, but just know that for some reason they may serve you. I think about all of the different areas of my life when I'm creating a new treasure map: health (physical and emotional), relationships, contributions, finances, skills and knowledge, family, identity, and what I am here to do. After I have a huge pile, I start to sort by those different areas and lay them out on a poster board. I also make sure to have photos of myself and my family. I learned nearly two decades ago from a friend how important it is to use

only photos of "heads" that you know. So, you may put your own head on Elle Macpherson's body (okay, that's what I did!). I also use my label maker to create specific goals; I type them on the label maker and then attach them to my board.

Using photos of yourself and loved ones is extremely important, as you'll see from the following story.

Nearly thirteen years ago, I had a big dream about writing a book. Now at that time most people who were

TREASURE MAP ESSENTIALS
Variety of magazines (mix it up—use gossip, money,
home decorating, food, travel, lifestyle)
Photos of yourself and loved ones
Scissors
Glue stick
Poster boards
Playful attitude

writing books were pretty much already well known. I
was just your everyday mom who wanted to help women
get back in touch with the gift of being a mom. I had no
idea where to start except with a treasure map. I cut out
words and phrases, typed up names of mentors whom I
wanted to write testimonials for me, and gave the book
a deadline date.

I was teaching an event in Los Angeles and decided
to show a group of my friends my treasure map. One of
my friends came up to me and asked, "Do you know that
mom and baby that you have posted in the middle of the
board?" I replied, "No, but isn't it a cute photo? That's
what the cover of the book is going to look like!" And my
friend said, "It will never happen." And I said, "Come
on, it's me, you know it will happen." But she told me
that it would never happen until I switched the picture

in the middle of the map to a mom and baby whom I loved and respected.

When she asked me why I decided to write the book, I told her that my passion grew out of my own personal experience as a new mother and that my son Josua inspired me. We then proceeded to North Carolina to shoot new photos, and after about ten rolls of film, we finally found the "perfect" photo. I then switched the picture on my treasure map with the new one of Josua and me, and two days later I received a book offer!

Everything I had put on that map happened. But when I looked at it, I didn't focus on all the things that covered my map. Instead I repeatedly asked myself, "Who do I need to become in order for these things to happen?" Reflecting upon this question helped me to figure out the specific steps I needed to take in order to realize my dream: I knew that I had to be resourceful in order to reach people for testimonials; I needed to be financially savvy in order to create a great press kit; I needed to be patient; and I needed to be a great role model of health and vitality for myself and my family.

Treasure maps do serve as a guide to finding yourself and what you truly want in life. And they encourage you to actively make it happen. Where is your map headed? That's up to *you* to decide. But in each of the following chapters, I'm going to give you a little direction and ask you some probing questions so that you have a good starting point for figuring out exactly what should be on your map. This is going to reinforce what you have learned—and really make every day fuller, brighter, and fun! Start now and have a blast!

Groove *n:*

1. A routine into which somebody has settled

Or how about: the idea that you're moving **forward;** *when you know that you're appreciating and using your gifts.*

CHAPTER 2

Moving Forward and Getting Your Groove Back

When I stand before God at the end of my life,
I would hope that I would not have a single bit
of talent left, and could say, "I used everything
you gave me."

—ERMA BOMBECK

When we're not true to our core, we feel as if we've lost our balance—or our *groove*. When we focus on what's wrong, and we no longer see the good in any situation, we need to find our way back—to get our groove back.

Let's look at Lisa for example. Lisa was living the life: She had her dream job, took great care of her body, and had an active social life. Then she started to take things for granted, pushed away those who cared most about her, started listening to the wrong people, and made some bad decisions. She lost her job, and now instead of buying designer bags, she is just trying to get by and pay the bills. She feels like she's caught on a treadmill of negativity and doesn't know how to get off. She's so busy dealing with the "normal" day-to-day struggles, that she's lost sight of the big picture. Her inner core has become dehydrated and is beginning to pull apart at the seams.

On the other hand, we know and see women who appear to have their groove on while in the toughest situations. One mother I know, Kim, was going through a not-so-ugly, but oh-so-painful divorce. A divorce is difficult enough, but on top of it, she was undergoing test after test to solve a serious medical problem and was unsuccessful in finding a full-time job. Anyone would crack under these circumstances! But through it all, Kim remained upbeat. Why?

Kim knew what her core beliefs were, and she was living them every day, remaining true to herself. Because she didn't have a job to occupy her time, she volunteered at her son's school. There wasn't a lot of money to go around, so she donated her time to various projects at her church. While waiting for job interviews, Kim honed her skills writing stories for her children. Keeping busy with the things she wanted and enjoyed doing kept her mind off of the bad things going on in her life. And that's when job offers began to pour in. The divorce was wrapped up and finalized. Her doctor finally figured out what was happening with her body and gave her a treatment plan.

Kim remained true to herself during the whole process. She didn't sit around and complain about what her life had become—there was little she could do about that. But she *could* take actions that were true to who she was, what she liked, and what she could physically accomplish.

The difference between these two women is clear: One decided to stop focusing on her problems and find a solution. Whenever you begin to lose who you are and feel lost in what you can do, there are four steps you can take to move forward:

1. *Put yourself in a better environment of people.* Kim went out and volunteered, finding contribution-based groups that would be a positive influence. Lisa should have sought advice from those who would offer support instead of listening to those who didn't have her best interest at heart.

2. *Start doing the things you love—access your gifts.* Kim used her writing skills. Lisa has excellent networking skills; she just needed to apply them in a creative way.

3. *Nip challenges at the beginning (kill the monster while it's young).* Don't wait until it feels like EVERYTHING is wrong—take each challenge as it comes. Kim tackled each issue one by one and didn't wait until she felt helpless to make changes.

4. *Focus on feelings that drive you.* There's a great
   story about a Cherokee grandfather and grandson:
   The grandfather tells the little boy that there is a
   terrible fight that goes on within each of us, that
   there are two wolves in conflict. One wolf is bad;
   that wolf is full of hate, anger, frustration, hostility.
   The second wolf is full of love, kindness, hope,
   faith, happiness, joy. The boy asks: "Who wins the
   fight?" The grandfather replies: "Whichever you
   choose to feed."

So which are you going to feed? Will it be the negativity, the lack, the scarcity? Will you continue to wonder why you don't have it? Why you'll never find a great
guy, get an ideal job, make the money you deserve? Or
will you feed the opportunity to have all these things?
Feed yourself with the feelings that will give you the
most joy; then you will see how much easier it is to find
the opportunities.

Personally I could have started to complain about
how hard it was to be a mom and about how many things
were on my plate that I simply didn't have the energy
or the time to focus on. Instead I stopped myself for
a moment and asked: What do I really want and what
kind of example do I want to set for my kids? And more
important, How am I going to get it?

Most women who feel out of balance love the idea of
finding their groove, but they don't know where to start.

They don't even know when or how they lost their groove to begin with, let alone where to try to find it.

The truth is, your groove may have been fading out for a long time, and you just choose not to pay attention to it. Maybe you decided that things were "okay for now."

Your groove may have diminished bit by bit over time without you even realizing it as you took on more responsibilities in your life. Maybe you had a baby, received a promotion, or began a new business venture. You became more and more focused on each of these changes and neglected your core needs.

But you need to make your *own* decisions about what is right for *you*. Ask yourself with every decision you make: Does this make sense to me? Whether your groove is buried under the motherhood role, the wife duties, the corporate persona, or financial strains, you can uncover it again.

Exercise: Getting "It" Back

1. Write down everything people thought you could never do. Now scratch the heck out of it. Now write down everything you've ever done when you thought you could never do it.

2. How can you empower yourself to move forward while it seems as if life is standing still, or maybe

even nudging you back? By using your gifts! Write down all of your special gifts, and remember that no one can take them away from you unless you let them. So hold tight to the *knowingness* of your gifts.

3. Think about something you've wanted to achieve, whether it's been a dream for ten years or ten minutes.

4. Write down what's been holding you back. What have you been feeling? What have others said that might have left you tentative to take action?

5. What's one little thing you can do to move forward? (You might want to find other women who are dealing with the same issues you are and talk with them about what you are reading in this book. You might want to get together with a small group of women who can bond with each other through the lessons in this book. If you want to learn how to plug into more amazing women, go to www.lobella .com.)

6. What personal gift can you use to accomplish that one little thing? How can you be creative and do what you love in order to get yourself going and get what you want?

Click on the Box That Describes You

Do you ever think about those little boxes you have to check when you are taking a survey, the ones that read something like this?

Check your age group:
- ❏ 10 to 18
- ❏ 19 to 24
- ❏ 25 to 40
- ❏ 41 to 55
- ❏ 56+

Don't you wish they were a little more honest, and asked you questions like:

What is your typical day-to-day mood?
- ❏ Feel great
- ❏ Happy some of the time
- ❏ Happy, then cranky
- ❏ Mostly cranky

Describe how you feel about your body:
- ❏ I work hard to feel great.
- ❏ I just need to lose a little weight.
- ❏ I can't fit into my skinny jeans.
- ❏ Let's not talk about it.

I was talking to a musician friend of mine a few weeks ago. As I was coaching him through an idea his band had, he said, "Loren, my target market is twenty-five to forty." Then it hit me: "Oh my God, I am not in that young, desirable market anymore."

I stopped for a moment to ponder that thought. And I have to be honest: I didn't know if I liked it or not. Being old meant that I was not as attractive anymore, not as useful in society, and that next week I was probably going to have to check myself into a nursing home. I was simply taking up space in a world that values those people in *other* boxes on the form, *better* boxes on the form of life.

Then I got back to my senses. Give me a break! *Thank goodness* I am now in the 41 to 55 age bracket. There's no way I could be writing this book authentically if I were in any other stage of my life. It's who I am as a woman now, and there's no place I'd rather be.

I have my groove back. I know my true passions. And I feel fully alive.

What age group do you belong to? Is there anywhere you'd rather be? Think back to each stage represented by those boxes and who you were during each time. Have you come a long way? Were you happy with who you were back then as a woman? Are there elements from some of those other time periods that you'd like to reincorporate into your life now? Perhaps you were more playful, passionate, or adventurous. Are you happy with who you are now, or have you lost your passion since then?

It's time to start figuring out just where you want to go from where you are right now—even if you truly think you'd be better off in another time of your life. You can't go back, you can only move forward, so you might as well think seriously about what you can change in your life now so that you feel more content, fulfilled, and fully alive.

The Four Stages

To know where we need to go, we first need to recognize where we are. I believe all women go through four stages:

1. *Discovery*: This is when you look for your real passion, what makes you tick (we'll dive more into our passion in the next chapter!). This process may happen for you when you're young (even as a little girl) or later in life. Sometimes we need to wait for our discovery phase, because we jump into what we think we're *supposed* to do and be instead of listening to what we *want* to do and be. This is the first step to learning about the real you.

2. *Stay true*: In this process there's a real certainty about who you're supposed to be; you *own* who you are. You're not comparing yourself to anyone else. You're living it every day—and not searching for things like you were in the Discovery stage. You are a little more

Amanda: A Journey of Recovery and Discovery

As an intern at a luxury hotel, Amanda was mentally and physically exhausted. She was dating a man who was good enough for now, convenient, but who became verbally abusive as well as demanding and jealous. He would control her and what she did; and Amanda allowed it because she felt that it was OK. She didn't realize yet what she would and wouldn't stand for. She gained close to thirty pounds in five months.

Then a new job brought big changes. Amanda was promoted to catering manager, her dream job. She no longer suffered from a lack of confidence, and she had a better sense of who she was and her mission in life. She now stood up for what she believed in. She broke off the relationship that didn't serve her. Once lost, she now embraced a time of discovery, learning what she really wanted for herself.

Though she was doing exactly what she always wanted, living the life she felt she was meant to, Amanda was tired all of the time and felt like her foot was on the brake and the gas at the same time. The doctors said the exhaustion and pain was an autoimmune disease (when your cells think they are the enemy and attack each other); she was diagnosed with lupus undefined connective tissue disorder.

Put on steroids, Amanda always thought, *There's gotta be a better way to do this.* I was holding one of my Lobella events—a program dedicated to building a community of great women and also helping women discover who they are—and Amanda was almost standoffish at first. What I didn't know was that she was insecure and doubting herself. But I watched her grow throughout the week and peel back the layers of what she had within her. She learned techniques to deal with her illness, and they gave her back the energy she had lost. With her recovery, Amanda could now continue the discovery she had started before being diagnosed.

selective in who you choose to be with and what you choose to do with your time; you're not willing to compromise integrity. There's an element of defiance here— you might not be popular with everyone all the time, but it feels good and right to you.

3. *Rediscovery*: At this stage you have finally let go of trying to make everyone else happy. When you finally pull away from that need, you get to stay true to yourself.

But at this stage you may also find yourself starting to compromise what you want because of a big life shift—a breakup, a new job, a death in the family. Pain often makes this stage a reality for many women. My friend Patty recently broke off her relationship with an abusive husband, then went through a series of physical challenges. But now she knows she will be okay—she has realized her gift, her real calling. She's no longer questioning if she will be able to provide.

4. *Stay connected*: This is where I am right now. This phase is about connection—and meeting more amazing people and situations than you ever imagined. You're no longer saying no to things; there's a real sense of opening yourself up to every opportunity. You also have a greater responsibility at this stage to take care of those around you. This is where the real revolution for women begins—when we really start to join together to make a change.

Understanding and knowing which stage you're in will help you determine how, and why, you need to get back into the groove of things. So which stage are you in? Is this the right stage for your life right now? If not, where should you be and why? What steps can you take to get to the phase that feels right?

Before we move forward, I want to acknowledge you for reading these first few chapters. I know I'm asking you to stretch yourself, but I promise you it's going to be worth it. Now let's talk about what's really going to fuel your life: your passion.

Passion *n:*

1. Any powerful or compelling feeling
2. The object of a fondness or desire
3. Strong amorous feeling of desire

Or here's another way to think about passion: You can't stop thinking about it; you're compelled *to do it. It's a contagious energy that you can feel oozing out of you.*

CHAPTER 3

Discover Your Passion and Feel Fully Alive

I was once afraid of people saying, "Who does she think she is?" Now I have the courage to stand and say, "This is who I am."

—OPRAH WINFREY

Sometimes we push our passions away, because we feel we can't justify doing something for ourselves. Maybe we wonder: How can I justify (playing tennis, painting, cooking gourmet meals) when it doesn't really serve my family? But trust me, pursuing your passions is a necessity, not a luxury.

You have to think of your passion as your reward. Your passion brings a richness to your life that you wouldn't otherwise have, and it allows your diamond to shine. When you follow your passion, your life is how you want it to be. You aren't following the direct orders of someone else; you aren't marching to the beat of another person's drum. You are living the life you were meant

Taylor:
KEEPING YOUR PASSION ALIVE

When I first met her three years ago, Taylor, my former assistant, was working at one of our favorite family restaurants in Portland; she had just graduated from college and moved up to the "big city" to conquer and accomplish. Since high school she had always known what her passion was: She loved to organize and plan, and she wanted to get into event planning. After living in the city for about eight months and trying to get her foot in the door any way she could, she started to get discouraged. She felt lost. She needed someone to trust her and give her a chance to gain the real experience she needed in her budding career. She finally found that luck when my friend Chris said: "I found the assistant for you!"

Working as my assistant, Taylor started to realize that she needed to just let life happen and not try so hard to control it. She knew she had to be true to herself and put her own happiness first. She did things that she never pictured herself doing, and she embraced it all. By pursuing her passion, and working with events, she finally began to look at herself for who she really was and begin a path of self-discovery. When we moved to

Nevada, Taylor decided to remain in Portland to pursue a relationship that was important to her, and she is now engaged!

Taylor still goes through her own peaks and valleys, just like anyone in life, but in those times when she starts to feel lost, she changes her routine and goes back to what she's passionate about. She'll pick up a favorite book that inspires her or create a new playlist on her iPod that keeps her motivated or call upon close friends for some quality conversations or take a trip home for a good family dinner.

She also wears a bracelet I gave her at a Lobella event; the inscription is "Stay True to Who You Are," and every day she wears it as a constant reminder to stay true to the woman she is and continue to live her passion.

to lead, engaged in the activities that leave you feeling energized and bring you joy.

Following Your Passion Means Taking Risks

Think about this story for a minute. Taylor didn't have a background in being an assistant or doing events, but what she did have was *passion.* In fact that's what made me want to hire her. She wasn't someone who was going to shy away from new possibilities and new adventures in her life. She was proactive and took on projects with enthusiasm (even if that meant just schlepping boxes and A/V equipment). She was willing to step outside of her comfort zone and go on the road, away from family and friends, for weeks at a time. She would make mistakes and then learn and grow from each new experience. Taylor did three things right:

- She knew what she wanted.
- She asked for it.
- She jumped into the job with the confidence that she could handle it.

By telling me that she wanted to get into the events planning industry, she took charge of her life and her happiness—and she's been successful ever since.

What if she hadn't spoken up? Would she have gotten the same results? The point is, she took a chance and made the connection.

Now you need to take some risks of your own. Let's get moving toward your Discovery process, or depending where you are in your life, your Rediscovery process.

Find Your True Passion
Think about the following questions and write down the first thing that jumps into your head:

1. What would get you excited to jump out of bed each morning? What would you do even if you didn't get paid for it? If you had no obligations in your life (just pretend for a moment), what would you do with your time? Go back to when you were sixteen—what were your dreams? What things just make your heart race with excitement and the hours pass without you even looking up? What passions have you had to let go of because you thought they were silly or you just weren't good at them?

2. Now, how can you make time for what you just wrote down? Who can help you realize this passion? How can you make it more convenient? (Want song lessons? Find a girlfriend who can do it with you. Want to learn more about yoga? Find out if an instructor can come to work during your lunch hour.)

Each of us has a fire in our hearts for something. It's our goal in life to find it and to keep it lit.
—MARY LOU RETTON

Lori: It's Never Too Late to Rekindle Your Passion

Lori discovered her passion at the moment it was taken away from her.

She started playing the piano at the age of five; she heard little tunes in her head that she could write when she was about six or seven. At age thirteen, because she was now more accomplished than her music teacher, she was set up to learn from a university professor.

But then Lori's father decided she would not pursue music. Feeling unsupported and abandoned, Lori decided she would never play the piano again. She spent many years feeling as if she had missed her mark, that she should have been a concert pianist. The loss broke her heart.

Twenty years later, after raising five children and starting a business and a successful career in medicine, Lori came to a crossroads in her life. With her youngest child ready to "fly the nest," she finally was in a place where she could really look at her life and what she wanted to do. But the idea of going back to her music felt unattainable; there was so much pain and so many unresolved wounds around playing the piano again.

She spent nearly a year wrestling with the idea of it. Then she came to slowly understand that we serve best when we are true to ourselves and pursue whatever it is that makes our hearts sing.

Today at forty Lori has moved past her fears; she is continuing her lessons and the endless hours of practice that bring her so much joy. Now in her Rediscovery phase, she is working toward the audition requirements for Portland State University's classical music program.

After hours of practice, Lori will sometimes go to the freezer to rest her sore hands and wrists on some frozen berries, and she'll see her favorite magnet: "It is never too late to be what you might have been."

NOW Is the Time to Find Your Passion

Through practice and the discipline it requires to do it, Lori found that she owns ALL of who she is and every bit of her own power. It has been a time of tears, frustrations, hope, joy—so many emotions, but all truly beautiful and all in the pursuit of rediscovering and once again owning her passion.

By now you should have some sense of your core and a few of the things that are part of your true self. Does your core include specific beliefs, favorite people, hobbies, interests, sports, or places you like to travel? Do you want your true self to include more aspects? Fewer? Of all the items on your list, how many serve as regular rituals in your life? Why not more? How many would you like to develop into regular rituals? Half? All? How can you accomplish this?

Continue to ask questions. You can be the woman who is always true to herself and her family. But in order to do so, you have to stop saying to yourself, *Oh, someday* or *I wish that were me.*

And once you decide that today is the day to take hold of your passion, that's when you start to feel truly alive.

Being Fully Alive: Authentic to the Core

Being fully alive means radiating from the inside out, experiencing the maximum levels of energy, vitality, and passion possible.

Answer the following questions:

- *What makes you feel the most alive, energetic, and vital?* For me, this changes. Sometimes just relaxing in the bath energizes me. Other times it's simply lying in bed with my family. It can be feeling the hot sun beating down on my skin, a good, long intense workout, or laughing so hard I cry! It CAN and should be all of those if you want to be fully alive.

- *How can you maximize your level of health, vitality, and inner and outer beauty?* Know that you deserve to feel healthy and vital from the inside out. Maximize your health by doing the little things that boost your energy and your spirit. This could be as simple as going outside and feeling grass between your toes, or saying to yourself, *Every day and in every way I'm happier and healthier.* Or the next time you're craving a treat, eat only half and throw the rest away. Take a bite and say, "I'm sweet enough!"

- *What are your unique qualities that not only cause you to feel good about yourself but that also make others notice you, too?* Are you quirky and playful? Or are you a leader, the one everyone goes to when a decision needs to be made? Or maybe you're known for your silent strength—you may not be the chatterbox of the group, but what you say has real purpose and meaning.

- *Who are you really at your core, and how can you take that to the next level?* Here is the bottom line: You are either living as a warning or an example, and I know that if you picked up this book, you are committed to being an example, so it is our responsibility to grow and continue to explore all that is waiting for us to embrace and be our best.

The Power of Rituals

Rituals are the foundation of every thing, and they can serve as a powerful source to reaffirm your passion and love and appreciate yourself more. Recent research has shown that the first ritual may have been performed almost 70,000 years ago in Africa (research that was done by a woman, no less, in Oslo, Norway). But what does that mean for you? Since the dawn of humankind, it seems that men and women have been trying to make sense of the world around them. The sun would suddenly be in the sky, and it would grow warmer, but then it would disappear again. To the prehistoric person, this didn't really mean anything more than a cycle of darkness and light, but in today's society, this signifies days passing.

In terms of rituals, these prehistoric people didn't realize that the sun was supposed to go up and down each day or that it was completely natural for there to be seasons when they couldn't grow crops. To help maintain some sort of control over these events, they used rituals. They celebrated when the sun came up and did simple rituals to pray for its return. There wasn't a sense of formality or even of pompousness, as so many of us regard the use of rituals today. These special times were simply used to create a connection between their world and themselves.

And we can do this now, too.

Who Has Time for Rituals?

Rituals can be as simple as reading the Sunday newspaper in the same location every week or cuddling with your partner for ten minutes in bed before you start your day or playing a specific song when you wake up in the morning. How old do you have to be to start rituals? Any age. You can keep the same one you've had since childhood, or you can create a new one at ninety years old.

Have you heard of the Delany sisters from New York? One of my favorite books was written by these lovely women, who never married and lived with each other well into old age. They wrote the book *Having Our Say: The Delany Sisters' First 100 Years* when they were 102 and 104, and it went on to become a best seller.

One of the things they wrote about was "Mama's time." When Mama sat in a certain place in their house, it was "her time." This space had a desk with a Bible on it. Over the desk was a picture of Abraham Lincoln and one of her family. When the children saw Mama at her desk, they didn't dare disturb her.

What rituals do you currently follow to make YOU feel good? One of my favorite rituals is taking a bath. Not only my family but also my friends and colleagues know that when I need to take a time-out and let go, I take a bath. It doesn't have to be long; it can just be a short bath. Once I am done, I know my groove is back. I think it has to do with being born in the year of the snake. The taking off of clothes represents the shedding of skin. I really enjoy and appreciate the sound of the water and the smell of the bath salts.

QUICK TUNEUP:
HOW DO YOU FILL YOURSELF UP?
What rituals do you follow to recharge your spirit? Are there new rituals that you can incorporate into your life to help nurture your body and soul? If you're having a little trouble with this quick tuneup, take a look at the rituals I've suggested below.

Create a Morning Ritual to Start Your Day
Rather than bouncing out of bed and right into the stresses of the day, start your day off right. When you wake up, lie in bed for a moment and start your day thinking about what's exciting about what the day may hold (trying a new smoothie for breakfast? going for a run with your best friend?). Then, when you get out of bed, put on a favorite song and just start moving, whatever that is for you—stretches, walking around, or maybe even dancing, (Remember Cameron Diaz dancing in her skivvies? Don't hold back!) Be quirky and have fun (no one's watching, I promise). Then you can start your

morning routine—and your day—with that right mix of energy and fun.

Start a Ten-Year Journal

Journaling has immense power to help you clarify your thoughts, be mindful of all that you are grateful for, and capture the magic moments of your life. One of the most fun types of journals is a ten-year journal. Every day write a few lines about what happened on that day. Then, the next year, return to the same day and continue writing. It takes literally less than five minutes, but the memories last a lifetime.

Pamper Yourself in a Luxurious Bath

Have you ever felt like the life was literally sucked out of you by energy vampires? It was! There are situations that happen daily in our lives that literally drain the life out of us. One of the reasons why I love this ritual is that it gives you the opportunity to just be with yourself, to reflect on the day, and to ask yourself what you are truly grateful for in your life. Think about all the people you love and what you are here to do. Then wait until everyone else in your home is asleep, light a candle, and just let it go. Lay still and listen to the love around you and within you.

Try this tip: Add Himalayan Sea Salts to your bath to fill you up. They have a very high mineral content, and you go to bed filled up, nurtured, and at one.

A Treasure Map to Your Passion

With all the things you *have* to do, it can be difficult to remember what you *want* to do—what really fills you up and makes you feel like a whole person (and a happy one at that). This chapter's treasure map will help you to remember those passions you've already come with, those things that really energize and inspire you, make you feel happy, and help point you in a positive direction.

Start thinking about the things you do that help you feel fully alive. What makes your heart race with excitement? What activities do you enjoy so much that the hours seem to fly by when you do them? What would you do if you had the day off from work or if money was no object? Your passion can be that little thing that brightens your day, such as baking cookies, reading a book, or making the time to go for a run. Or it can be a larger passion, such as taking a class, writing, painting, or spending more time volunteering.

Put on some soft music, close your eyes, and allow yourself to daydream about what you most love to do. Picture every little detail of what it would feel like to do that thing and revel in the feelings of being completely satisfied and content with the world and the passion you LOVE.

What does your passionate treasure map include?

Great *adj:*

1. notably large in size
2. large in number of measure
3. remarkable in degree, magnitude, or effectiveness
4. full of emotion
5. used as a generalized term for approval

I prefer greatness *—the innate ability to be more, do more, and see more than you think you are capable of.*

CHAPTER 4

Step into Your Greatness

What are you willing to let go of in order to step into your greatness? You may be saying to yourself, Me? Greatness? Yes, YOU, and yes, GREATNESS!

Why do we make it so hard for us to win? I believe the longest journey we'll ever take is moving from our head to our heart. Why? Because it's so easy to get stuck in our mind, to make sure logic defines all that we do. Because that's what we're supposed to do, right? Not necessarily! When we lead with our head all of the time, we don't really "live" life, because we're always trying to figure out what makes sense instead of embracing the spontaneity of creating moments. But I'm here to remind you what you already know—what your heart tells you. Sometimes you have to surrender and let go of how things "have" to be! Lighten up; you don't have to do everything just "right." (And did you ever stop and think: "Right" by whose standards? And are those the standards I want for my life?) So many of us are great cheerleaders for everyone else; maybe we need to stop beating ourselves up for all the things that "aren't perfect" and start being

Linda: OPEN TO POSSIBILITIES

Linda had been in the same job for about six years. It no longer fulfilled or excited her, or gave her any growth, and she was desperate to do something different. She felt she was living a half-hearted life. But she didn't really know what she wanted to do, and although she loved the idea of working for herself, there was too much uncertainty in setting out on her own. The doubts ran through her head: What if no one gave her work? What would she do for money? What she didn't realize was that she was limiting her horizons by listening to the fears in her head instead of following her heart and dreaming big.

So finally, feeling frustrated and empty, Linda decided that she would stop beating herself up and just be open to new opportunities. She threw herself into a year of learning, contributing, and meeting new people. Immediately she began to open up. She realized she had been limiting herself by being so focused on what she *should* do, rather than what she really *wanted*—to travel the world and make a difference in people's lives. How many times are you so focused on one thing that you don't notice what is really going on around you?

But at the end of a year, nothing had changed. And the months continued to pass. She felt stuck. Do you ever feel that you just don't know what to do to get started?

And then a fabulous opportunity appeared: a job offer for which she had no training, background, or experience. Within a few weeks she was in New York, then Australia. She worked at events with thousands of people and managed life-changing seminars. In less than a year everything had changed. When she stopped worrying about what was practical and sensible, she opened herself up to a possibility that she could never have imagined.

At first she found herself a little overwhelmed in her new role, trying too hard to prove herself, grasping at control to feel more certain, and following rules that weren't hers. Do you ever make things harder than they need to be for yourself? And when she began to just let things happen instead of pushing to make them happen and plugged into who she really was, her team started to connect with her and respect what she had to say. When she got back to her real core and stepped into her greatness, not only did she feel fulfilled and happy, but that was when she crossed over to her Stay True phase and *really* got to make a difference to other people.

our own cheerleaders so that we can peel back the layers and discover our greatness.

When you do decide to lighten your load, your greatness will be revealed. Greatness can be found in the littlest things; greatness shines when you stop trying to push things and you just *are* and open yourself to new opportunities. It's a celebration of all you are—inside and out.

Embrace the Greatness within You

There are three things you need to do to step into your greatness:

1. Love and appreciate yourself
2. Nurture your body and spirit
3. Make an agreement with yourself

Let's get started on the first thing.

First you have to decide to own yourself and own your core like it is something you have waited so long to have and you finally got it! It's yours and no one can take it away.

O – Open to the possibility that you are all you need

W –Wanting more isn't selfish

N – Never settle for anything that's not true to you

Y – You can do anything and be anything
O – Owning your decisions is power
U – Understand what you like
R – Recognize your beauty every day
S – Stop criticizing your decisions of the past
E – Engage yourself in an inner positive dialogue
L – Leave doubt at the door
F – Free yourself of any guilt

Richard Bach once said that at the end of your life you will be asked only one question: "How much did you love?" How much do you really love the good times, the bad times, the hard times?

Speaking of the hard times, I remember after having my third child that I was really frustrated with my body and I disliked how I felt. All of my "personal development stuff" was just not working, so I came up with the "And" Opportunity.

QUICK TUNEUP:
THE "AND" OPPORTUNITY
Ugh my belly is so flabby after my third baby!!
AND? And I want it to be flat!
AND? And it's not!
AND? And I want it to be.
AND? And I need to take that
Pilates class so I can have it!

This exercise motivated me to take action and DO something to love myself (rather than be resentful) and embrace every part of my life. Quick tuneup: Take out your journal and try this exercise for yourself!

Commit to Taking Care of Your Body

We've all started off the year with promises to be better to ourselves, usually in the form of New Year's resolutions that somehow get thrown out with the champagne corks the next morning. We have the best intentions, just not the best actions. (We also need to realize the importance of having the right support and finding that one person who will hold us to our commitment and our intentions. Sometimes all we need is someone to push us—I once had a friend call me every morning to tell me to go to the gym!)

If you really want to maximize your energy, your vitality, and your passion, you need to start taking care of that body many of us so often neglect. When your cells are happy, your brain is happy, and you can begin to live your life eager to try more and do more. If there's one thing I've learned as a nutritional therapist, it's that in order to feel good emotionally, you MUST feel good physically.

Here are some great ways to start making healthy changes to your life (and get that energy and vitality that you need every day!):

- *Eat more fresh and organic produce everyday.* There's no excuse not to eat more fruits and vegetables these days. Even the biggest grocery marts carry some organic produce that is fresh and bursting with photonutrients, vitamins, and minerals. Adding more produce to your diet is going to help your body and your beauty.

- *Drink more water, preferably filtered.* Our bodies are 75 percent water, and in order to keep everything running well, we need to replenish our water "supply" throughout the day (our bones are one third water for goodness sakes!). Breathing alone lowers the amount of water in our bodies. Commit to drinking a glass of water when you first wake up, one in the mid-morning, one at lunchtime, one in the afternoon, and one at dinnertime for starters.

- *Add more activity to your life.* Do something, *anything,* for exercise during the day. Skip to the park and hop on a swing, or you can just walk around the block for thirty minutes a day to get your blood flowing and your skin glowing. Instead of jumping into your car during lunch, walk down to the local deli or shopping area. (At one six-day event that I teach, I always head at least once to the merry-go-round across the street; I pretend it's my *Sex and the City* moment and strut the whole way!) This doesn't have to feel like work—just getting up and moving will make a difference!

- *Cut out the junk food.* That's right, you knew I was going to say it. Junk food is just that—junk. You need to look at what you're fueling your body with. And while I enjoy a sweet treat every now and then, having sweets as a part of your daily diet just isn't good for your body, your mind, or your skin. Sugar breaks down the collagen in your skin. Stick to foods without preservatives and you'll find that your skin is brighter and healthier than it's ever been.

People are like stained-glass windows. They sparkle and shine when the sun is out, but when the darkness sets in, their true beauty is revealed only if there is a light from within.

—ELISABETH KÜBLER-ROSS

You Have to Take Care of Yourself

Think of yourself as a glass of water. When you give something to yourself that you enjoy, like a nice walk in the park or an hour of uninterrupted reading, you are filling up your glass and everyone can have a sip. But when you don't take the time to take care of yourself, you're pouring that glass out, leaving nothing for yourself or for anyone else.

Bobbi Brown: CREATING BEAUTY

Bobbi Brown is a name that many women know well. Her makeup line is focused on creating beauty in anyone, not creating something that is false or forced. By allowing women to discover the parts of themselves that they love and want to celebrate, she has created an empire based on bringing beauty from the inside to the outside.

But the real question for me is not whether she is a role model, but whether she is someone who takes the time to care for herself. By helping women around the world find their beauty, is she a person who is taking the time to do things for her own inner beauty?

Without being her best friend, I think that I can safely say that she is a woman who has a firm grip on her groove—she knows exactly where it is.

On a 2007 Oprah show, Bobbi said, "[T]he most important thing in life is health. If you take care of yourself, you can do anything."

So she does. Yes! A woman living her truth!

You need to take care of yourself in order to take care of others.

Love Yourself One Day at a Time

God plants us each in the right garden, I think, a place that presents just enough sun and rain for us to take root and grow, creating families, bringing together the right people to teach and to learn the right lessons.
—CAROL LYNN PEARSON, CONSIDER THE BUTTERFLY

Whether you realize it or not, you're probably addicted to helping others. When we're not doing something for someone else, we feel like we're not needed, so we seek out chances to overextend ourselves no matter how hard it is or how much we don't have the time, money, or energy. But at what expense?

Think about it: When was the last time you took some time just for yourself? And I don't mean those five minutes that you waited in the carpool lane at your child's school. Or waiting on line at the grocery store, skimming through trashy magazines. Really, when was the last time you took time to nurture yourself? When was the last time you really loved yourself?

For my thirtieth birthday a good friend of mine, Monique, presented me with a box of index cards with handwritten notes of what people loved about me. Now

A Contract to Love Yourself

One thing I do to commit to loving myself is to sign a contract with myself. You sign contracts with your clients to get things done, so why not sign a contract with yourself to make sure you start loving yourself enough? (Like my kids always tell me: "Mommy go help lots of people and take care of you!") Pull out your journal and write the following:

I, _____, promise to begin to put myself first from now on. This means that I will start doing things that I enjoy each day so that I can . . .

(Make a list in your journal of all the things that make you happy, such as taking a long hot bath, listening to James Taylor music, or looking at the sunset. Turn back to where you did this in Chapter 3.)

I will commit to loving myself more for a period of at least thirty days, starting on _____ ____, 20____.

At the end of this time, I will be happier because I know that I deserve to be loved—especially by myself. This contract can be renewed at any time because I should never stop loving myself. Then sign and seal with a kiss!

when I'm having a rough day, maybe doubting myself, I will pick up one of the cards that someone wrote, as a reminder to love and acknowledge myself. Here's something simple you can do: The next time you receive a thank you card, keep it on your desk for at least the next week. See that card as the gift it is, a reminder that someone loves and appreciates you.

You deserve to start making a commitment to yourself and to your happiness (isn't that what we teach our kids?). Your happiness may be slipping away from you because you just aren't taking the time to look for it anymore. And part of celebrating your greatness and claiming your inner beauty begins with making the promise to love yourself.

Step into Your Greatness

Stepping into your greatness means declaring to nurture, support, and love yourself first; committing to a lifelong journey of growth and spiritual evolution; appreciating and enjoying the process at a deeper level; resolving to contribute and give back wherever possible; joining the sisterhood of women committed to supporting each other and making a difference in our homes, our communities, our countries, and the world.

Really think about the following questions:

- How can you celebrate your personal greatness?
- What are some ways you can send a ripple of love,
  happiness, faith, or gratitude into the world?
- What is important to you as you continue your
  self-discovery and evolution as a woman of
  incredible inner and outer beauty?
- In a world full of unpredictable events, tremen-
  dous pressure, and unprecedented change, how
  can you ensure that you stay true to who you
  are?

Let's face it: It's so much easier to stay in our heads
(but it's much more fun to stay in our hearts!). Our jobs
want us to be logical, predictable, and productive. Our
families have lists of things that need to be done in
order to be "finished" for the day (is the work really ever
done?). But in the end, we wind up feeling more overwhelmed than we were at the beginning. So why would
we do this? Why would we want to set this example? It
is time to stop pushing ourselves to the back burner. I
don't know about you, but I think my self-discovery was
pushed right out the window and onto the lawn! But the
truth is, I let that happen . . .

You must create a space in which you can be your
own unique version of your greatness. And each version is different. You need to start looking at your life to
see where you can fit in YOU. You can't expect another

person to make you great and complete. I learned this lesson many years back with my husband, Shore. When we got married sixteen years ago, we both came into the relationship complete. But then we tied the knot, and for some reason we started to compromise to make each other happy . . . because that's what we thought we were "supposed to do." I stopped going to meet girlfriends at the gym after work, or parties on weekends, and Shore gave up opportunities to go out with his buddies and windsurf. We started to shrink away from who we really were, because we thought that's just what you do! We lead with our thoughts rather than our hearts, right? And we didn't communicate openly, because we were afraid we would hurt each other's feelings, and it just kept getting worse.

Then we started to get resentful. I had our first child, Josua, and felt like I was doing everything—working and taking care of the baby. So I wanted a divorce. And all of this happened because we never told each other how we truly felt. I felt like a shell of a woman, and he didn't feel like the man he once was (strong, independent, and clear about what he was here to do). Though we had come into the relationship whole, we had become only halves of our former selves, because we thought we were supposed to fill each other up. That's the reason people get married, I thought, so they can be complete, bring on a new dimension. But you can't do that until you're whole first.

I needed to get me back as a woman; meanwhile Shore needed to get himself back. I realized I had to stop expecting someone else to fill up my life to make me happy. I encourage you to get back to your real self. When disagreements happen between you and partner, ask yourself: Is this really about your husband or boyfriend, or is this because you've lost sight of who you really are? Then think about ways you can get back to you (flip through some of the exercises you've already done in previous chapters for ideas).

We were separated for nine months; during that time I got back in my flow, and Shore began to feel more confident and attractive. One day we saw each other—and it was like when we first met! We went on a "first date" and started over, as complete individuals. Now we step into our greatness as a couple and as individuals. Our relationship is better than ever, and we are celebrating twenty years since we first met!

How to Create a Vision for Stepping into Your Greatness

Businesses have vision statements that help guide them to their profit goals. But in this far more amazing journey of self-discovery and finding your beauty, passion, and greatness, you deserve one, too. In order to craft your own personal vision statement, begin by asking yourself the following questions and recording the answers in your journal:

1. Who are you at your core? When are you at your best? How do you show up? What about who you are makes you proud?

2. What are three nice things you can do to nurture and take care of yourself within the next thirty days? Write down what you will do, why you are committed to doing each one, and by when you will complete it. You already did this in your contract, didn't you?

3. If you could reinvent three things about yourself, what would they be? What new qualities do you want to explore, deepen, or enrich within yourself?

4. One of the best ways to expand who we are is to do things for other people. Think of five people in your life whom you cherish. Write down one thing you will do within the next two weeks to show them how much you care.

5. What are some social causes that make a difference to you? What beyond yourself and your family would you like to give to?

6. What are some of your spiritual beliefs about life? About death? About love? About happiness?

7. As you look toward the future, what are you most excited about? How do you envision your life during the next year?

8. What are some things you want to do during your lifetime? Brainstorm a list of things you'd like to see, do, touch, taste, or experience. Include some silly things as well as a few more lofty goals.

9. What are some of your most cherished memories from your life so far? What have you experienced that made you happy, fulfilled, proud, grateful, or full of love and joy?

10. What do you commit to do in your life that will ensure that you stay true to who you are? What support system can you set up to help you to bring out and continue to be your authentic self?

Top Rituals for Stepping into Your Greatness

By introducing rituals into your life, you set up a sacred space in which you can begin to find out who you really are. You're going to start finding beauty in everything, and eventually you will find beauty in yourself as well. Fall in love with yourself—you're your own soul mate. The following rituals can help you to be more mindful and to honor the person you are—and the one you wish to become.

Transform Doubt into Good

Doubt comes when you feel *I'm not good enough.* Doubt is what freezes you from moving. Even if you take action with doubt, it really is poor action. The key is to focus on what you *do* want rather than what you don't want. Focus on something bigger than yourself and consider: *Maybe this is part of my path, and I can share it and become more from this experience.*

Do a Reality-Check Ritual

Once you finally begin to achieve the goals you've aspired to your entire life, try to fully accept where you are in the moment. Instead of rushing, pushing, and essentially creating more chaos for yourself and others, take a few moments to experience the beauty of the realization of your dream with the following ritual:

1. *Miss the action.* Allow yourself to sit in a place for a few moments without disruption. Incorporate more quiet and serenity into your day. If you had planned on visiting three museums in a city you are visiting, you may visit only one, take a nice long walk, and sit in a café instead. Allow for the beauty of the day and the gratitude for where you are to catch up to you.

2. *Mute your mind.* We all keep running commentary in our heads, hoping that words will make what we see more real. Instead, take a moment to release thoughts on how things "should be" or how you always "dreamed it

would be." Allow yourself to actually live in the moment and just be.

3. *Close your eyes.* Though we usually take pictures to make an occasion special, we can also fix the impression forever in our memories by closing our eyes and savoring the moment with our senses. Allow the sounds, sights, images, and feelings of love penetrate every part of who you are.

4. *Write a letter of gratitude.* When the day, ritual, or visit has ended, write a letter of gratitude to all of those who helped you achieve it. Then write a letter to yourself. Recognize and celebrate all you did to get where you are, and make a list of your "favorites" of your visit, including other souls who touched your life and how.

Create a Ceremony of Annual Renewal

Create a ritual to prepare for the New Year. Journal about who you will become in this next year and what that will mean to your life. Try some of the following activities to start the year off:

- *"I am" box*: Fill a box with fun words to describe yourself (use the adjectives you came up with in Chapter 1!), and throughout the year pick out a word every so often. For example, if I pick outrageous from my box, I'll go and do something spontaneous and crazy (we'll talk about the pole dancing class later!).

- *Bury disagreements*: I believe something good always comes, even from something bad. So if you've had a fight with someone in the last year, plant a tree or do something positive to wipe the slate clean and start the next year fresh.
- *Family treasure box*: Load a box with treasures for your husband, kids—and yourself! I load my box with treats for the kids and Shore (including date-night coupons), and when one of my boys gets straight As, or Shore gets a speaking gig, we dip into the treasure box. It might sound corny, but the box is a really great way to get enthusiastic about your goals for the year.

Think about it: What's one thing you can incorporate into your life to get excited for the New Year? (And don't think you have to wait until January 1—you can start any time you want.)

Write Your Once Upon a Time

Write about your life or a piece of it that you don't understand and would like to. Write it as a fairy tale or a short story. Begin your story with, "Once upon a time . . . " or "It was told that . . ." Include an obstacle that has yet to be overcome, an encounter that has significance, the gift you received or the lesson learned, and how you triumphed in the end (I love this one).

Practice the Art of Forgiveness
Write yourself a letter of forgiveness. It can be for big things or little things, but include anything that you have hung onto that you need to release. Be sure to put yourself in a space of compassion and kindness and imagine the freedom and peace it will give you to let go of these things once and for all.

Plan a Vacation
The Latin root of the word vacation means "freedom." We all need time and space to rejuvenate, play, and fill ourselves back up. The key is to make sure that in addition to any fun, adventurous, or more extravagant travels you have in mind that you also take time for a holiday that is simply for *you*. This could be a day at the spa or even a quiet day at home alone to read a book or watch a favorite movie—whatever will give you that feeling of taking a break from the world and from your responsibilities.

Talk to Your Body
The body houses the soul. Write about your relationship with your body. Do you love or abuse it? I have a friend who turns to sweets every time she gets stressed. Acid craves acid, and since stress is acidic, it craves acidic foods such as caffeine, sweets, or cigarettes, but sugars age the body quickly. Instead she needs to come up with an empowering alternative for dealing with stress, such

as going for a run, taking a yoga class—or even knitting. Write about what you could do or are already doing to have a healthy relationship with your body.

Make Space for New Things in Your Life
Take some time to make room in your life for new things, ideas, and relationships. To do this you need to clear the way! I had a friend who after breaking up with her boyfriend of nearly five years threw away everything that reminded her of their old life together—well, almost everything. She couldn't let go of this one box of Christmas decorations. She held on to that box for years—until the day she went on a first date with a man for whom she knew she had to let go of the past. After all, only then could they have a new life together.

So, make room for new opportunities! Every day for the next nine days, give away twenty-seven items (nine is the number for completion; twenty-seven, 2 + 7 equals nine). According to Barbara Biziou in her book *The Joy of Ritual,* by consciously doing this, you will prepare for changes in your life while invoking the spirit of gratitude and generosity.

Cleanse Your Soul
Only after we release ourselves from old beliefs that create barriers for opportunity and fulfillment can we can renew our hopes, aspirations, and dreams. Loving yourself and appreciating others are key to achieving your

goals in life. Take time to become aware of whatever is out of balance in your life and to put in the corrections. Take an inventory of your life so that you can see the changes you need to make to make each day happier and full of beauty. Write down in your journal anything and everything that has been bothering you, or holding you back. Then next to each thing, write down one thing you can do to make yourself feel better about the situation—how can you see the good in something that once was painful?

See Life through the Eyes of a Child

If you've had the gift of spending time around a young child, you have probably noticed that they have a completely different perception of the world than most adults. They are insatiably curious about everything, they are quick to forgive and forget, and they find joy in the simplest things. To a child, an empty cardboard box is an enormous castle, a pile of dirt is a great place to play, and a mother's lap is the safest, softest, most wonderful place in the world.

If you aren't around children in your daily life, find an opportunity to connect with some—volunteer at a children's hospital or school or offer to babysit for your sister-in-law.

Before you move on, commit to doing at least one or two of these rituals of stepping into your greatness.

Are you beginning to feel that brilliance come back a little bit? Are you starting to understand that these things bring a depth and clarity to your life, and a deeper sense of meaning? Before we move on, open your journal, stand up, and take five minutes to review all of your hard work. Say your "I am" statements out loud. Say what you'll stand for. Yell out your passions. How does that feel now?

Strength *n:*

1. The physical or mental power that makes somebody or something strong
2. The ability to withstand force, pressure, or stress

Or, how about: A confidence that comes from within, that allows you to speak your mind and take on any challenge.

CHAPTER 5

The Gift of Your Gentle Strength

There is nothing as gentle as strength, and nothing as strong as gentleness.

—FELICITAS CORDOVA APODACA

What does gentle strength mean to you? To me, it is the ultimate gift of being a woman. Think about it: We can be the nurturer and the disciplinarian, we can be powerful and understanding, and there is beauty in it all! I believe that *gentle* strength, not just strength, has really allowed me to step into who I am and be firm and compassionate and powerful and feminine all at the same time.

I was at an event when a woman came up to me and said: "You and my trainer are examples of 'gentle strength.' But I can't have both; I have to choose . . . I just *can't*." As I watched her I thought: What does she need to know? She needs to know she is being heard— from one woman to another—and that I am going to listen to what she really needs. I asked her, "When you see me, what do you see?" She started to cry and said she didn't know.

Then I asked: "How do you want to feel?"

She said: "Like you feel; I can see how carefree you are, while at the same time you can command a room with your heart. How can I do that?"

I looked her in the eyes and said, "Think about something bigger than yourself, think about what your girls would want you to feel. It's your choice. How do you choose to feel?" I told her that I choose to embrace both so that I can be a great example for my kids and other women.

But why does there have to be a choice? As women a lot of times we *think* we're forced to choose between being strong or being vulnerable. But think of classic examples of gentle strength over the years: Princess Diana, Rosa Parks, and Jackie O. And think of modern examples such as Melissa Etheridge, Sheryl Crow, and Mariane Pearl. What do they all have in common? They are women who never compromise, who always carry themselves with elegance, grace, and a confidence that can not be shaken.

Connect to Your Gentle Strength

So what makes a Rosa Parks or Sheryl Crow? What are the elements that allow you to discover your gentle strength?

- *Speak up.* Stand up for what you believe in. Like the example I gave in the introduction of this book, I needed to find my voice as a twelve-year-old girl in order to find my quiet strength. No one can take that away unless I choose to give it away. (This is a huge part of this chapter, and we will go into more detail later on.)

- *Be willing to listen.* Knowing when to hear what another person has to say is just as important as knowing when to speak up. That's why God gave you two ears and one mouth. It's a clue. I have learned the power of listening from my husband. He is such a powerful example of gentle strength in a man. He doesn't have to "do" anything to be a "man"—he just IS. He isn't always talking about himself, which makes him a bit of a mystery, which then makes him more powerful.

- *Be patient.* You don't need to know all the answers right now. Just be confident in what you do know, and know who you are at your core. One of my favorite exercises, which I learned from my friend Joseph, is called the STOP technique. Whenever you feel you want to react to something,

STOP **T**ake a big deep breath Think about your **O**utcome **P**raise yourself for not reacting!

- *Be persistent, but not overly aggressive.* You don't need to push yourself and others all of the time (that is just exhausting and irritating at the same time!). Things start to flow naturally if you simply allow them to happen. When you come across too strong, sometimes people will choose not to listen—mostly because they feel you aren't listening to what is important to them.

- *Project a quiet confidence.* When everyone else is panicking during a stressful situation, remain calm and collected. You will be the person everyone turns to in a tough situation. One of my favorite photos is a picture of a lighthouse, a storm, and a massive wave smashing the lighthouse. If you look really closely at the photo, you can see a man standing at the base of the lighthouse as the wave crashes on the other side of him, three stories up. If you look even closer, you can see he is actually relaxed, holding a cup of coffee.

A beautiful example of gentle strength and being the calm in the storm is my good friend Michelle.

Michelle: A Quiet Confidence amid a Storm of Change

The last two years had been a major turning point for Michelle, and she felt her womanhood/ motherhood/wifehood at another level. Within a few weeks she experienced more than some of us experience in a few years: Her daughter Ava was born, her mother suddenly passed, her family moved to a new home, she changed jobs, and she turned thirty.

Michelle had no choice but to be the calm in the storm, maintaining a sense of normalcy and togetherness and serving as the rock for her family. She had to make a decision not to lose it and that her family would not only survive, but come out the other side thriving. She was fighting every day to make sure her family had the basics—food, shelter, health care, and education (she went before the board of her daughter's school to request a scholarship for her daughter to start kindergarten). She was focused and determined, and she used the grace she had within her to provide for her family and to be an encouraging, strong example for her husband, who was having trouble finding work.

When chaos crept in, Michelle dug deep. She knew she had gentle strength and that it would keep moving her forward. Through it all she has realized that part of her quiet determination is to be humble, kind, loving, caring, and compassionate. She had a trust and confidence about who she was as a woman, and she knew how to show up during tough times and be an example for her children. As her mother always used to say: "Get up, brush yourself off. Put on a little lipstick — it will all be OK!"

How to Regain Your Gentle Strength

So it's time to ask the hard question: What's holding you back from fully experiencing your inner power and strength? My dear friend Brenda (who epitomizes the idea of gentle strength) has great advice for how to regain your gentle strength:

- *Acknowledge this power you already have within you.* Look back on what you believe were your most difficult times. Be silent and still with yourself and reflect on how you managed during those situations. There were things you said and beliefs you had at those times that you didn't even realize were guiding you . . . that is a big piece of your gentle strength. Realize that you, and your silent strength, pulled you out of those times.

- *Nurture your relationship with yourself.* Gentle strength is possible for everyone. You must first and foremost be committed to an open and honest communication with yourself, and you must trust that you will follow through and put yourself first when necessary. The more consistent you are with checking in with yourself, the easier it will become. And because you will be an even happier you, those around you will be as well.

- *Trust your heart.* Gentle strength lies at the core of every woman. It consists of knowing what you want and need to do and following your heart or your intuition. Gentle strength allows you to love yourself (even with the imperfections you think you have) and to spread that love to others. Gentle strength can guide you in obtaining your outcomes, showing your love, and helping loved ones in times of illness.

The woman I mentioned at the beginning of this chapter, who felt she couldn't feel her own inner strength, needed to acknowledge what she already had within her, and she had to trust what was already in her heart. She left my program with a new sense of who she was and what she could do.

> ## QUICK TUNEUP
> Now take some time to think about the gentle strength within you, and what may be holding you back from fully feeling that calm power. Spend ten minutes writing down everything you think could be stopping you from realizing your full potential. What steps can you take to really own your quiet confidence?

What's Your Juice?

One of my favorite metaphors about life is from Wayne Dyer. He asks: When you squeeze an orange, what comes out of it? Juice. What kind of juice? Grapefruit juice? Tomato juice? Apple juice? No. Orange juice. When people squeeze you, what comes out? Anger, frustration, tears, or love? If all that came out of you was good, how would that feel?

When we are squeezed past the point of exhaustion, when people try to squeeze more and more out of us, what is going to happen? What kind of juice are we going to make? It's probably not going to be something sweet and refreshing if we are totally sapped of energy.

But how exactly do you find out what kind of juice you are making with your life? How do you change the juice that you give to everyone else? For me, it was a matter of finding out who I was and what I enjoyed in my life. A good exercise for rediscovering yourself is to write in your journal every night with the prompt: *What did I learn about myself today?*

The answers will amaze you. Some days I found that I didn't like something that I'd told myself that I *did* like and vice versa. For example, once when I was on the road, the only thing on television was pay-per-view opera, and I thought to myself, *never mind, I don't really like the opera.* But then I said, *what the heck, I will just watch it.* I was amazed with how relaxed I felt, and how inspired I was by the performers' voices, costumes, and bodies! As I became quiet and honest with myself, I began to notice that the person I was to the world wasn't always consistent with the person I was inside. No wonder I was having trouble finding my groove—I was forgetting who I was.

Try this exercise for even a few days to see how many things you learn about yourself. But don't stop there. When you begin to find new things you enjoy and that inspire you, go out and explore them more deeply. Take classes, read books, and talk to others with the same interests. By simply taking the time to discover yourself, you will begin to find out what you need to create *your* ideal life. It's like Glinda told Dorothy, "You always had the power to go home." So do you. You can go home to who you really are. When you do, you will feel more love, happiness, and satisfaction when people squeeze you.

Rituals to Cultivate Your Gentle Strength

Knowing others is intelligence; knowing yourself is true wisdom. Mastering others is strength; mastering yourself is true power.

—LAO TZU

What rituals do you need to instill in your life so that when people squeeze you, you will be able to stay true to who you are? Here are some rituals you can use to harness that elegant strength and quiet confidence that I know you have in you.

Speak Up

You never hear that a relationship—with a friend, a coworker, a lover—broke up because of too much communication! Quite the contrary is true: Most relationships end because of a lack of communication. We allow the fear of potential consequences step in, or maybe we are just too chicken to speak up.

But here is the real question for you: What did not speaking up in the past cost you? A friendship? A job? A relationship? Your self?

I once met with a woman because everyone said I should meet her. They thought her company had the potential to be a sponsor for my events. We met, we had a great time, and I said to her, "I will be speaking at a conference in a few weeks. I would love for you to come and get more of a reference for who I am and what I am about." But then I never heard from her!

A few months later, I went to a trade show and there she was. She seemed distant, and I thought to myself, Maybe there was something there I didn't know about. A few days passed and I decided to call her. I was honest and asked, "Hey, it seemed we had a great rapport going and were really connecting. What was going on?"

Her reply blew me away. "I am a cheap banker, and I can't afford to go hear you speak!" I told her I wasn't expecting her to pay for a ticket, I was going to pay for her! It was as if a huge weight had been lifted off her shoulders. Sure enough, we scheduled a meeting to see how we could work together.

Sometimes I think we tend to shy away from speaking up because we don't want to hurt anyone's feelings.

The lesson here: Speak up! But if you've never really spoken up before, you need to learn how to do it first:

- *Notice other people's body language.* When people face you and look at you, they *want* to talk to you. They *are* listening. Too often when we talk with people we create scenarios that aren't really happening. But when we notice other people's body language, we can see what their mouths may not be saying. If a person is turned away from you, this isn't necessarily a sign that you need to be quiet, but rather that you need to be a little more persistent until the person does turn to you.

- *Lower your voice slightly.* When you lower your voice, it can help steady your mind as well as your thoughts. This will help you as you begin to talk to anyone, plus it has a calming effect on the other person, helping him or her to feel at ease when he or she talks to you.

- *Be up front about how you feel.* When you start off your sentence with, "This is something I really feel strongly about," you will get someone's attention immediately.

- *Ask questions to make sure that you have all the facts.* Repeat things you hear from the other person in order to be sure that you have correctly heard what he or she has said. Also, ask questions of the person to whom you are speaking to ensure that he or she heard what *you* said.

- *Be persistent.* As in the example I gave above, sometimes you need to be persistent if you want to be heard. After you talk to someone, follow up with a phone call, an e-mail, or a handwritten note. This will establish that you are interested in talking and that you are going to be persistent about communicating.

- *Realize that your ideas are important.* It's easy to think that our ideas don't have merit or that we are simply wasting someone else's time. But don't think that way. Instead, try to look at your ideas as though they came from someone else. That can help you see how important they are and that they deserve to be shared with someone else.

Out of the suggestions above, choose the one you need to work on most—and then do it.

Help Me to Speak Up Ritual

I've always found rituals useful in my life and in my personal growth. By creating a sacred space for myself and my thoughts, I not only tap into my feminine power, I also tap into my confidence and intelligence. You might call it "collecting your thoughts." I call it "summoning my self to action."

A ritual that I do to give me the courage to speak up is quite simple—it's one you can do anywhere, any time, without anyone being the wiser. When you need to speak to someone, or you need to bring up a point that you feel is very important, here's what you can do:

- Take three deep breaths to help steady yourself.
- Push your weight onto your toes if you're standing up. This helps to keep you from shaking if you're nervous.

- Then say to yourself three times: What I have to say is important and deserves to be heard.
- Then begin talking.

If you have to talk to someone but are having trouble summoning up the courage, even though it's very important to you, the following ritual will help you feel self-empowered and ready for anything:

- Write down everything you want to say to the person you need to speak to.
- Read it to yourself to make sure it says what you want it to say.
- Read it to someone you trust to see if he or she understands what you mean to say.
- Read it over and over to yourself before your meeting or your phone call.

This repetition will help you find the true power behind the words you want to share. By reminding yourself again and again why your message is important, you will feel powerful and ready to *speak your mind*.

You are a woman who deserves to be heard. By speaking up and being curious about the world around you, you can begin to speak the words that have been trapped in your soul. You can show the world your precious voice.

A Treasure Map to Your Gentle Strength

Found your gentle strength? Great. Now that you've rediscovered it, what can you do to hold onto it?

This is another way that treasure maps can come in handy. By helping you focus your energy in one direction, you can begin to understand how *you* view the world in relation to who you are as a woman. This map might include images of what you consider to be gentle or feminine—flowers, light colors, soft fabrics, and so on. You can also add images of what you consider to be strength—maybe it's a strong mentor you had or pictures of historical women who projected an elegant power—anything that reminds you that you have it within you. And make sure to add a picture of you with all of these elements!

The purpose of this exercise is to map out what you perceive to be your version of being a woman—a healthy, sensual, vibrant, and powerful force.

You go, girl!

Balance *n:*

1. Something used to produce equilibrium
2. The remainder or the rest of
3. The ability to decide an outcome by using one's strength and influence to one side

I think it's a lot easier than all that — it's having everything that will make you happy, whatever that is!

CHAPTER 6

Balance It All— Have It All

Life is like riding a bicycle. To keep your balance you must keep moving.

—ALBERT EINSTEIN

Did you ever go to the circus as a kid? Remember the guy who could balance and spin six, seven, eight plates at once . . . while juggling a torch of fire? Those plates would all spin at the same time, until he noticed that one of the plates was spinning out of control. When he tried to compensate for the one prop out of synch, everything came tumbling down. Have you ever noticed that when you focus too much on one area that all of your "plates" start to fall?

My friend Cynthia was committed to having it all and making sure all her plates were spinning in unison. She was successfully juggling her children, her coaching business, her health and fitness, and her involvement in her spiritual life, until one day her husband seemed to need more time. They started to spend each weekend away to be with each other. Of course, the first disagreement occurred and then the next. Then the evenings turned into talking things over and working things out. Before she knew it, she wasn't working out or going to her Bible study or visiting her children or spending any time prospecting for new clients. The relationship plate had teetered, and in her effort to grab/save it, all the other plates had toppled.

Cynthia realized the imbalance and took action. She reconnected with her friends and began to spend time with her children. In addition, she went after new clients and went on morning walks. The result: She felt terrific about who she was and was full of life. It was possible to reengage in real conversations with her husband and reclaim her marriage. Balance—and the idea of having it all—was part of her life once again.

Having it all means clinging to all the areas of life that are important to you; declaring that you can and will create the life of your dreams; honoring all parts of yourself and your life; discovering how to create the ideal balance that achieves your goals and fills your heart; and becoming an example for all of what's possible. Having it all is the feeling of being filled up and seeing that the facets of your diamond are both bright and polished!

Some people say that you can't have it all (I say their diamond may be a bit murky!). I think that when you make a conscious effort to honor the unique diamond that you are, stay true to yourself, and pursue your goals, you can achieve an incredible sense of joy and satisfaction in your life. To get you moving toward your own version of "having it all"—where you have that sense of ease and synchronicity—you first need to answer some questions honestly.

- What are all of the parts of your life that are important to you?
- What if you could tap into your resilience and resourcefulness and still feel a sense of peace, balance, and fulfillment?
- What does it mean for you to "have it all," and how can you achieve it effortlessly?

Your Definition of "Having it All"

When you think about "having it all," what does that mean to you? Does it mean a successful career that you enjoy, as well as plenty of quality time with your family? Does it mean having enough time to exercise and feel good about yourself every day? There are no wrong answers here, only those that ring true for you.

I work with one woman who can't wait to get married (she's recently engaged) and have a baby of her own. She yearns to give up her high-powered job and be a stay-at-home mom—all of these pieces mean "having it all" for her. But then I also know a woman who is thriving in her professional life and traveling (solo) all over the globe; this is her version of having it all.

Pull out your journal and think about what your ideal life—or even ideal day—would look like. The first step in making it happen is having a vision of what's most important to you. I mean *really* important to you. How do you want to feel every day? Every day I wake up and decide in advance that today is going to be the best day of my life. You *can* have everything, if you follow a few fundamental steps: Use your qualities or talents, have a clear vision, work smarter, schedule balance, have the right strategies, and believe in the power of rituals.

Utilize Your Top Qualities

We all deserve to "have it all"—great health, a loving and supportive family, a passionate relationship, a wonderful career, access to spiritual growth, positive bank accounts, and an opportunity to contribute to something meaningful. It is up to us individually and collectively to make this happen. What are the qualities within you that will you allow you to achieve all of the things that are important to you (the definition you just worked on above)? Think about what you wrote down in previous chapters and how you can use what you already have to create the life you want.

MISSING: MY BALANCE

Found my balance?

My balance will respond to "serenity" and "peace"

Loves to get things done for others

But still makes time for myself and my interests

Will have plenty of sleep and a rosy glow

Craves Me Time

But doesn't obsess about the details

Is consistent with my core values

And always says "No" when it means "No."

Have a Clear Vision

Have you ever had a dream and told someone about it, but that person said, "No, no, no—you can't do that; you have to do it THIS way!"? You can't listen to that person. You know what feels right, and you have a vision for what it looks like! I firmly believe in the power of visualization and intention to create our own realities. When we can begin to envision our own success, we can create the life we have seen in our dreams. By planting these images in our minds, we begin to manifest them.

Remember: You need to take action, too. My friend John Assaraf, author of *The Answer*, founder of One Coach, and featured in *The Secret*, said there was one thing they left out: You can put out your intention, but you need to actually put your attention on it, and not only that . . . you must *do* something that will get you closer to your goal. A great example of this is my friend Amy, who had a dream to buy a house by the age of thirty. Every day she would envision herself coming home to her "sanctuary"—but she didn't just leave it to her mind to make it happen. Every month she wrote down why she wanted the house, charted the monthly amount she had to save in one year, and then looked at this chart regularly. Within the year, Amy had purchased the home she had always wanted: a three-bedroom, three-bath condo. A vision—and a plan—helped her achieve her goal by the time she turned twenty-nine. Because she made that vision a reality, she now has a reference for how she can make anything happen.

> *Our intention creates our reality.*
> —WAYNE DYER

Visualize Having It All
Start visualizing ways to enhance your life so that it feels more balanced and you feel more fulfilled. It won't happen all at once with pixie dust, but it will start to flow with a lot more ease, and you will get momentum in your life. Think about the following questions. See if they help

you imagine what aspects of your life you need to work on and realize those that already seem to be working.

1. In what ways do you already "have it all" in your life? What are you grateful for, proud of, or happy about with the way your life is now? If you say "nothing," ask yourself what you could be happy about.

2. What are all the areas of your life that are important to you (health, relationships, finances, emotions, spirit, career, and so on)? Which ones do you spend the most time working on? Where do you spend the least time? Which ones need more focus in order to create the balance you desire?

3. List one or two female role models whom you aspire to be like. It could be a friend, someone in your community, or anyone else you have met or heard about. In what ways do you feel they have it all? What can you learn from them or model to create more synergy and balance in your life?

4. One of the best ways to have it all is to let go of some things that no longer give you much value. What are some things in your life that no longer give you the joy or benefit that they used to (for example, a club membership, an extra phone, or a

subscription service you never use)? What could you do instead that you would enjoy more?

5. Think back to when you were a little girl. Who were you then? Were you more hopeful or positive? More active? More playful? More adventurous? Is that little girl still present within you today? Are there parts of her that you miss? How can you nurture that part of you?

Work Smarter

You can have it all—you just don't need to personally *do* it all! Recognize all of the ways and resources you have to do what you want. Ding, ding, ding!!! This is the thing that I have learned that has really transformed my life. *I don't really have to do it all? But what if someone does it differently than I would? Oh, I actually might learn a new way to do something? I may lighten up and enjoy the things I do like to do???*

A crucial piece: You need to have a schedule that works for you. I have read many books and attended many seminars, and here is what I can tell you: Not one schedule is right for everyone, but there are some principles that work whether you are a president of a company or a mom. The art of balance comes from creating a schedule that enables you to focus on each of the primary areas of your life but that also allows for flexibility.

Chris: GIVING AWAY YOUR GIFTS

I met Chris Love in 1993. We immediately formed a deep connection through our love and desire to create and help others. We spent hours brainstorming ways to change the world, one project at a time, and weekends serving meals and clothing to homeless people. That same year, Chris met a wonderful man, whose name is also Chris, who she would eventually marry. He was in his sixth year as a professional basketball player. At the time, he was the only player in the National Basketball Association with type 1 diabetes.

With my friend Chris's passion for volunteering and her husband's desire to give back to the community, they formed the Chris Dudley Foundation. The foundation focuses on helping people live active lives while living with diabetes. My friend quit her job and poured herself into helping her husband. She recognized that Chris was overwhelmed. He had a disease that demanded his attention twenty-four hours a day; he played a game that demanded physical and mental strength; and he was barraged by people wanting him for autographs, money, and his time. Chris committed herself to be the one person in his life who wanted nothing. She wanted him to know that she loved him for him and not for who he was or what he had. For many years she gave all of her energy to making his life easier.

As the Chris Dudley Foundation grew, she helped start the Chris Dudley Basketball Camp for youth with diabetes. The success of the camp, and the fact that it was the only one of its kind in the world, helped gain international attention for her husband and the foundation. My friend continued to handle the public relations, set up his appearances, coordinate major fund-raisers, and write all of his speeches. She sat back and watched his star rise, somehow finding time to give birth to three children in three years, each born in a different state! They were very busy people!

After a sixteen-year basketball career, Chris retired from the NBA. My friend still continued to manage many things for her husband. But one day Chris woke up and apologized to her husband. Over the last several years, she had silently been harboring resentment toward him because he was taking everything she was giving to him. Being angry at him would not make things better. She explained the importance of rediscovering herself to her husband. He agreed to help make that possible by sharing more family responsibilities.

Now that she knew what she needed to do, she came to me about *how* to rediscover her identity. I asked her to follow the same steps I outlined for you in this book, and she is now in the Discovery phase. She has made great strides, and I am proud to say that she just finished writing her first children's book about overcoming adversity. She is happier and healthier than ever before.

Schedule Balance

It's a funny thing to think about, but you really DO need to schedule balance into your life. While most of us have been taught that we need to balance our schedule, it's actually the other way around: We need to schedule our balance so that we can really enjoy and not stress so much about things.

In order to do this, you need to realize that you are worth the time it will take to change your life into something you love waking up to. After my first son was born everyone told me how "different" my life was going to be and how it would never be the same again. At the beginning, when I had my new little baby in my arms, I worried about whether I would ever find time for myself again, because people told me I wouldn't. But looking into that little person's eyes, I realized that in order to be the parent I longed to be, I needed to make the time to be the best woman I could be. And that meant taking some time that was mine and mine alone.

It doesn't have to be much, but it does need to be consistent. As I've evolved (at least, I'd like to think that I have), this time has changed. But it used to be that I would take fifteen minutes or so every morning simply to sit with myself and a steamy mug of whatever sounded good that day. No mommy duties, no work responsibilities, just me and my mug. I'd look out the window and notice the light changing the sky from darkness to pinks and purples, and I'd remember how blessed I was to be who I was and where I was. This little ritual focused me and my day with me in mind. I wasn't living for anyone else in that moment; I was living for me—and it made all the difference.

Live and Love All Areas of Your Life
Now let's make this practical so that you can develop not only a schedule but a way to embrace and love all that you have to do without feeling overwhelmed.

I used to have a big yellow pad with a list of everything that HAD to be done. One day I noticed that I felt a bit resentful about this, and thought to myself, What do I want to do and why? If you ask yourself this same question, it will create a powerful change in the way you approach your life. Ask yourself the following questions:

- What do I want?
- Why do I want it?

- How do I get it?

Remember: The most powerful question is the *why question:* Why do I want this for my life?

I'm a big believer in Tony Robbins's RPM system. The R stands for results, or *what* you want. The P is for purpose, which is *why* you want it. The M, or Massive Action, is *how* you do it. Most people live their lives by what they want done and how to do it. They typically miss out on life because they miss out on the *why*, the real connection that gets us excited to do things.

It is also important to categorize your life into bite-size, more manageable pieces, called "chunks." If we try to take in everything at once, we feel overwhelmed and don't enjoy what we're doing. When's the last time you tried to shove an entire cheeseburger into your mouth? Did you like it? So why would you do that with your life? You've special ordered this life, so why not take pleasure in each part of it?

I've got four chunks I focus on each week:

1. Me

2. My relationships (family and friends)

3. My work

4. My contribution

I commit to always paying attention to these four pieces. I'm writing this book and teaching an event, away from my husband and boys (the babysitter is here with me and my daughter), so my focus this week is really on my work. But that doesn't mean these other pieces fall off the list. If anything, it gets me to pay more attention to them! For example, I'll send my boys a care package, or I will text my husband throughout the day; as for taking care of me, I meet the sitter and my daughter when the program isn't in session, and I take a bath every night and make sure I take mental breaks throughout the day.

I've found that if I don't plan for each category, then I have to take whatever comes my way and I feel overwhelmed. I also risk not making time for what matters most in my life or work out for thirty minutes.

I realized as a mom how much I have started to learn again. When we "do" our lives, we sometimes stop thinking and just "do." When my kids ask, "Mommy, why is it important to . . . " or "Mommy, why do we need to exercise every day?" I actually have to think again and not just "do." I have the opportunity to think about how exciting things are and how blessed my life really is. Asking yourself why is your premium fuel for the day; it helps get your creativity and vision going for your life. The why enables you to come up with all the cool reasons to take action and move forward in your life.

STACK YOUR "WHY" REASONS

Remember the "And" exercise from Chapter 4? Let's use it again and this time make it about the why example I just did with a friend who is frustrated with her weight.

I am committed to losing 20 pounds.

Why?

I'm sick and tired of not wearing cute clothes.

Why?

I want to move easier and be able to kick the ball around with my kids.

Why else?

Because I have an amazing body, so why am I abusing it and not giving it what it needs?

Why else?

I remember the fun I used to have when I exercised.

Why else?

I'm ready to feel sexy again and put on the sleek dress sitting in my closet.

Why else?

Because I deserve to feel healthy and sexy all of the time.

Now it's your turn . . . .

Regardless of what I have going on, I plan my week every Sunday at 6:00 p.m. No exceptions. I'll plan in the bathtub or in bed, and everyone knows that this is "Mama's Planning Time." It's like brushing your teeth twice a day—something that is a must—because I know what an impact it has on my life and the lives of everyone around me.

The first question I ask: *What are the most important things for me to focus on this week?* (Notice that I don't immediately ask myself to list all of the things I have to get done this week.) I always put me at the top of the list (because you've got to make you the priority). Then I look at family and friends. I focus on the relationships part (with myself and others) first. When that's in order, I feel good about whatever I'm working on and feel congruent, whether I'm speaking at an event, writing a book, or coaching someone. Relationships are the base of all I do.

Next I think about what I want from each of these areas for the week. For example, for myself this week: *To be committed to doing something for my body, such as working out.* (Depending on what's going on, another week may be about rejuvenation or refueling my spirit.) Then I go to the why: *Because I've been blessed with this body, I know all the things I need to do to nurture my spirit and physical body; there are so many great resources available to me; I want to be a great example, someone who walks their talk.*

Then I move to my next category, family and friends. And I repeat the same process. *My outcome this week is to continue to be the best forever family friend—a caring, loving friend, wife, and mother—and continue to be the heartbeat of my relationships.*

Why? *Because look at how blessed I am; I'm able to create because of the support of my family/friends. And I have an obligation to let them know how much I care about them.*

I'll read through the first two categories again and get re-associated with what I want to do and why. Then (and only then) do I start scheduling the week and writing down my to-do items.

So now it's your turn to use this system. Keep it simple and remember to include these four chunks:

1. You

2. Your relationships

3. Your work

4. Your contribution

Make sure you group everything into these four chunks (how good does it feel to boil down your entire life into just four areas?!) What about finances? Or paying the bills? These are all linked to your relationships, or maybe you consider them your work. Do whatever works for you!

Anne: PRESENT FOR THE MOMENTS THAT COUNT

For my friend Anne, having it all means being present. In a perfect world we would do one thing at a time—but as we all know, that just doesn't happen in today's lightning-fast culture. Anne has found that being present and enjoying each moment give her a greater sense of peace. For example, when she picks up her daughter from school, she won't get on the phone with the office. She will spend the five minutes on the way home in the car truly with her daughter (not just sharing space), asking questions, singing, letting her talk. Five minutes may not seem like much, but it makes a big difference to her. Those are five minutes with her she didn't have before, because she was too busy trying to fit in other things and then wondering why she felt like she didn't have the time to be a good mother.

Another important ritual for Anne is family dinnertime. She has finally arranged her schedule to allow her to get in a full day and be at home to make dinner. She chooses not to work at that sacred time of the day. She realized that preparing food for her family and sharing it with them at the table is more important than being the last to leave the office.

Anne understands that you can't have it all unless you are grateful for it all—even if it comes all at once. She thinks about life and balance as a meal: Each course is better when it is savored on its own, eaten in the order it is served.

Now write down the result you want from each of these chunks—what's your outcome for the week? Then write down why you need to get this result; what are the compelling reasons behind each outcome? When you've given yourself a big enough why, you'll always find a way to make what's important to you happen. Then you can start to schedule your week, building in appointments, meetings, and everything else. Make sure to come back to your plan at the end of the week and note in your journal the differences you experienced!

Find the Right Strategies

We are now going to dig into strategies. I know, when I first heard the word strategy I thought: *Ugh, we're going corporate—not another strategic planning meeting!* Hopefully you'll have a more enlightened approach for the following strategies.

Most people use strategies or tools on a regular basis, but they're simply not conscious of what they're doing when they use them. Also, many of those unconscious strategies don't work very effectively, but we keep doing them over and over again, because they are so ingrained in our subconscious.

We need to wake up and get conscious with our strategy building, because a strategy is really a formula for doing something successfully. I have worked hard by myself and with others for two decades to uncover the formulas that work— the ones that save time, money, resources, and more important, emotional angst or frustration. The other exciting piece about strategies is that once you develop a strategy in one area of your life, you can then apply that formula to other areas. For example, I might work on a plan to communicate and connect with my child that motivates and causes him to feel loved. Well, that same approach will often translate to a coworker or one of my best friends.

So it's time to have some fun uncovering formulas that can help you have less stress, more results, and HAVE IT ALL!

Focus on What Matters Most
Instead of thinking that everything is pressing and needs your immediate attention, realize what is truly important to you. I know you are thinking: *But what about all the stuff that has to be done?* Do this process first and I will

show you how it takes care of itself. You might even want to write a list each morning of the most essential things of the day.

Remember You're in the Right Place

Just as I sit with my mug in the morning, tell yourself that no matter where you are, no matter how rough things seem, you are in the right place for this particular moment in your life. It may not feel like it now, but later when you look back on this time you may realize that it taught you something important or brought someone valuable into your life.

Tap into the Power of Rules

Create rules for yourself about how you are committed to living and the things you will not stand for. After doing so, you can begin to make decisions based on these rules. For example, if you don't want to go out every night of the week with friends or business associates, because you wind up exhausted and depleted, make a rule that you spend at least one night alone each week to recharge.

Be Resourceful So You Can Do What You Love

When you take the time to focus on the things you love, the rest of the world can take care of the rest. For example, if you like to write, then write. If you want to spend this time uninterrupted, have someone watch the kids or simply turn off all the phones, cell phones, computers, and so on until you are done. The rest of the world can wait. If you're financially strapped and can't afford a babysitter, see if you can work out an arrangement with another mom in which you watch each other's kids. Think about how else you can save time—I hate to do laundry and find it takes up too much of my time, so I use the wash and fold in my neighborhood. I simply drop off all of my laundry and pick it up a day later, all ready to be put away. This frees up my time and enables me to focus on the four chunks of my life that mean so much to me.

Utilize the Power of Dreams

Dreams aren't just for kids, you know. Be sure to always have dreams of things that you want, things that you hope to do, and goals you wish to accomplish. And with those dreams, you can make plans and take action. When you stop having dreams, life can feel monotonous and lack meaning.

I remember nineteen years ago driving with my mom and saying, "Mom, let's do this whole goal-setting thing." My mom said, "I'm too old to dream!" I pulled the car over, and shall I say, we "had a little discussion." Since then, my mom has accomplished more than she ever could have imagined and has realized dreams she may have just given up on.

Create a Wish List

Remember when you used to make wish lists for your parents for the holidays or your birthday? Make a wish list for your life right now so that the universe knows what you want from it. Besides bringing positive energy your way (you've got the hang of the "law of attraction" by now, right?), studies show that the act of writing down your goals also makes you that much more likely to accomplish them.

My list of things that actually happened is longer than I ever could have imagined. Every year for the past two decades I have written down that I wanted a "house in Tuscany." On my fortieth birthday four years ago, we were in Vegas, where we had decided we were going to move. I left with my friend to go to New Orleans to help with the Katrina effort. My husband stayed in Vegas to find our new home. He called to tell me he had found where we are going to live . . . in a community called "Tuscany." Of course I had meant Tuscany, Italy, not Tuscany in Henderson, Nevada! But I love it and am glad I ordered it up!

Stick to the Basics

Instead of being complicated in your life, try to remember that the simple things matter most. I wake up and appreciate sunshine that hits my face in the morning, or when my daughter, Asher, smiles. You don't have to follow a certain religious path or do complicated rituals. All you need are the things that make you happy.

Expand Your World and Ask for Help

While it's tempting to stay cloistered in the trenches of your mind, your world can become enriched by those around you. Try talking with others who share the same interests as you, or ask for help when you are having trouble managing everything in your life. You might be surprised at just how willing others are to help you (think of how great you feel after giving a gift or sending a package). In fact, think of it as allowing another person to feel the joy of giving. When you try to do everything yourself, you deprive others the joy of offering their help.

Banish Judgment

There is no right or wrong way to do anything, so instead of thinking that you're headed in the wrong direction or you're not doing things properly, remember that each step can be a step away from what you don't want in your life. And that's a step in the right direction.

Take Time to Celebrate

Too often we neglect to tell ourselves just how proud we are of the things we've accomplished. There are so many awesome ways to celebrate. It could be as simple as stopping before you move on to the next thing that needs to get done to tell yourself, *Great job,* or treating yourself to a nice dinner or a massage. What's important is that you do something to acknowledge a job well done!

No one has ever measured, not even poets, how much the heart can hold.

—ZELDA FITZGERALD

Embrace the Power of Rituals

Rituals help you carve out your life even further so that you feel less of the anxiety or stress that tends to creep into day-to-day life. They allow you to focus on what's truly important, and they create a rhythm that supports the balance you need in your life.

Master the Art of Appreciation

Appreciate everything and you allow more good things to come into your life. Instead of always wanting more, try to realize that everything in front of you right now might be enough. Each night write a list of all the things you appreciate. This activity will help you foster a sense of gratitude and focus more on the positive than the negative in your life.

Create a Monthly Date Day with Yourself

We take spouses and partners out on dates, why not ourselves? To begin the romance with ourselves, we need to make time to be with things that we love, with the person we love—our self. Create a day for yourself when you will do something to nurture yourself—whether it's a day at the spa, a walk on the beach, or simply window-shopping alone. You don't have to spend money, and you can be creative—perhaps volunteering at a soup kitchen will nourish your soul.

Reclaim Your Youth

Life can be serious, but it's at those times when we need to be silly, too. Try heading to the playground or exploring some hobby that you used to do as a child. Take a walk and collect interesting leaves or get out the paint and some paper and get creative. Or, grab some friends or family members for a game of softball and a barbecue. Make time for some fun in your life!

Nurture Your Creativity

When people hear the word *creativity*, they often think they need to paint or draw. But creativity can come in many forms—knitting, writing, doing puzzles, taking classes, cooking, and so on. Find one way each day to be creative in your own special way.

Write a Thank You Note

Thanking yourself as well as others is a great way to become that woman you admire. When you take a moment to appreciate others, you show that their actions have not gone unseen. Of course, writing yourself a little thank you note every now and then can be just the pick-me-up you need.

Imagine the World the Way You Want It to Be
Instead of focusing on all of the potentially negative things in your life, try to shift your attention to the world as you want it to be. For example, in the morning before your day begins, review your schedule in your head. Create the perfect chain of events as you imagine it to be. You will be surprised at how easy it is to create the perfect day when you use your imagination first.

Release Guilt
No matter what you do or don't do, someone is not going to agree with you. As women, we have been taught that this is a cardinal sin, that we are somehow less of a person because we can't please everyone. Pleasing everyone is an exhausting process—and a race that cannot be won. When we try to please everyone, we become guilty, and for what? Instead of drowning in guilt, make decisions about what makes you happy. And if someone else isn't happy about your choices, that's not something you need to worry about anymore.

Dare to Break the Rules
Women have been taught that they need to live this way or that way in order to be acceptable. But rather than following these rules, try to break them. Instead of sitting in silence next to a woman in line at the drugstore, try talking to her about a funny story you heard. When you begin to break the rules, you might just make someone's day.

Let's do one last ritual, a quick tuneup, in order to continue the momentum toward balance in your life.

QUICK TUNEUP

At your core lies what you believe in, what you value, and what you need to be happy. This is your creed. When you stop to "read" your creed and to memorize it, you are able to make decisions that are truly in line with who you are and can remember why it's so important to make time for who and what you love. Write down your creed and post it on the wall or on your desk to remind you to stay true to yourself and your beliefs.

Space *n:*

1. a period of time
2. a limited extent in one, two, or three dimensions
3. an extent set apart
4. the distance needed from other people or things in order for a person to feel comfortable
5. an opportunity for privacy or time for one's self

Or how about a sanctuary? A haven *that nurtures your core, and allows you to tune in to your true self.*

CHAPTER 7

Create an Energy of Happiness in Your Space

I long, as does every human being, to be at home wherever I find myself.

—Maya Angelou

Have you ever caught yourself saying, "Ugh, I just need my space."? You do need your space—we all do! Even our pets do. Personally, I have noticed that now that I have created a space that makes me feel fabulous, I am able to contribute more, because I feel good while I am creating. It's not just in my home, it is everywhere I go! I know what makes *me* feel awesome.

Take a moment to look around you. Whether you're at home, in your office, or somewhere else, when you look around you, do you feel good about the space? And I'm not talking about whether the room is warm or cool enough, whether the space is big enough or well organized. I'm talking about whether your environment makes you happy.

In your life, you want to find your groove and reclaim your happiness, right? But when you surround yourself with things that don't make you happy, how exactly are you going to be able to accomplish this? How can you be happy when you don't feel happy where you are? You now have the opportunity to redefine and express who you are and who you are becoming.

Though you already know that you need to define who YOU are in order to find out how to make yourself happy, what about your personal style? When you start to define your personal style, you can begin to create an environment that INSPIRES you to do more, to BE more. Refining your space is a creative process. As you revamp your space, you will notice something new ignited inside of you.

And remember, the most important part of this process —the purpose behind your re-design. Remember in the last chapter when we talked about the power of "why" you want to do something? Think of all the compelling reasons why you want to change up your space. What will it mean for you? How will it make you feel? What will it mean for your family, your friends? What other areas of your life will it impact? (Here you might want to take out your journal and do a Stack Your Reasons exercise for your space.)

Creating Trueness in Your Home

I remember when we moved into our present *home,* and I do mean *home.* It was the first time that it didn't feel like I was just living in a *house.* I was committed to making sure that I opened the boxes outside my home and only brought in the items that I loved and made me feel great. Your home offers you a unique opportunity—a place to fully express your grace, sweetness, lovingness, and ability to uplift and serve just by how you set up your home and decorate it—and do it for YOU! You set a subconscious imprint to all who come to your home as to what you stand for, who you are, and how you want your relationship to be. Is your home going to be a place to restore your soul and remind you of your purpose, or is it going to look and feel like a place that tries too hard to be the way you think people want you to be? Is your home going to feel congruent with your soul, or is it going to represent debt and financial stretching to keep up with your neighbors? Is your home going to make you feel as though you have arrived at a place designed and projected to provide safety, security, and calmness after a long day out, or it is going to be a place that drains you and your soul (and not to mention everyone who comes for a visit!)?

Think of the great homes you have been to and why they left an impression on you—not because they were wealthy looking, but because they felt good, warm, loving, and intentional.

In order to be great, you are required to be you. You need to represent you in your home and create a connection among you, your soul, your intention, and its manifestation. It is perfect training. If you can accomplish this inside your home, the lessons and habits you learn will ensure that you are successful outside of your home as well.

One of your goals during this life tuneup needs to be the creation of a home that is nurturing, peaceful, and happy. This is your "home base," where you can come back and find yourself supported—no matter how tough things get. You should walk in the door to your home, relieved that you are there. Your home should be a place where you are true to yourself. If you can't be true in your own home, where else can you be yourself? In order to create this environment, you need to think about how you will create your space so that it fosters this joyful energy.

Creating Your Space: The Energy of Happiness
Creating your space involves setting up your life so that you feel nurtured, happy, and at peace; harnessing the energy that surrounds you to help you to create your dreams; awakening to the impact of textures, smells, and beauty in your environment; and defining your personal sense of style and utilizing it to take your life to the next level.

Answer the following questions as truthfully as you can:

- When was the last time you paid attention to or nurtured your personal space?
- How conscious are you of the impact of your physical surroundings on your personal energy, health, happiness, and success?
- How can you transform your space to feel better, reduce stress, and flow seamlessly from one area of life to the next?

Your Definition of Creating Your Space
If you had to define what your ideal space looked like, what would it be? Would it be cozy, with lots of soft textures and colors? Or would it be bright and energetic? Would it have lots of photographs of people you love— or framed prints by your favorite artist? Would you have scented candles or fresh flowers? Think about all the different elements that you feel would make your space a cozy place that would make you feel inspired and relaxed. Whenever I travel, I make sure to bring my ideal space with me: I bring a picture of my family, my kids, and my husband; a great quote in a frame; my travel journal; and relaxing oils and candles. They always stay packed in my suitcase, so I don't have to worry if I packed them or not.

Your Top Qualities
Your personal space is one of the elements that defines you as a woman. What traits can you tap into to harness

energy, reduce clutter, and beautify your life? Are you really creative, good at leveraging to others, a great researcher, an obsessive organizer, or a decorating queen? What qualities and skills do you enjoy using to create your space? Write down your strengths and how you can use them to create a personal space that brings more energy and happiness into your life.

Your Vision for Creating Your Space

Just like you need a vision for your life, you need a vision for your living environment and a home that nurtures, inspires, and reflects who you are—and serves your needs. Without a clear vision of who you are and what you want, it's easy to stumble around in the dark.

For the next ten to fifteen minutes, take out your journal and brainstorm the vision of what you want your space to be. Start with some of your favorite things—what are the colors, sounds, smells, and textures that excite you? What parts of your personality do you want to make sure shine through? What do you love to do, and how can you make sure these activities are represented? Then think about other spaces you've been to or seen that you would love to model—maybe a neighbor's home, a storefront, or maybe something you caught on HGTV! There is no limit on what can inspire you. Just write. You may find that you will discover things you never knew made you happy!

And then let's consider your current space:

1. What is your favorite space in your home? Your bedroom? Your home office? Your kitchen? Your workplace? Why? What energy does it give you?

2. What space gives you the least energy, pride, or joy? What area in your physical environment do you feel takes energy from you or needs the most work?

3. What changes can you make in your personal space to tap into the appropriate energy to help you achieve these goals? For example, what would happen if you replaced your grandmother's hand-me-down sheets with a new, luxurious, high-thread-count cotton? Would it entice you and your beloved to spend more time in each other's arms?

4. What physical space is in most need of an overhaul? A messy desk? A disorganized closet? A nonfunctional kitchen? How much stress does this add to your life, and what would happen if you were to transform this?

5. Look back through the other parts of your journal. How can you support these areas of life utilizing your physical space? For example, what if you

put out fresh fruit and vegetables on the counter every day? Or replaced your water and air filters? Or redid your bath so it enticed you to relax every night?

6. Think about other women in your life who have things in their environment/space that you like. Who are two or three people you can meet with to exchange ideas? What do you want to model from them? How can you support them, too?

7. Choose one area in your home that will be your personal space. What can you do in this area to help make you feel good about yourself, inspire you, or give you peace?

8. What three new decisions can you commit to make right now that will make the biggest difference in this area of your life?

Make Your Home Your Altar

For many people, the idea of a personal altar sounds a little hocus-pocus, but it shouldn't. A personal altar is simply your own personal space in which you can place anything of importance to you; your altar is where you find peace, balance, harmony, and grace amid everything going on in your life. In his book *Altar Your Space*, Jagat Singh Khalsa talks about the importance of making your home an altar and to be "surrounded by beauty, to know peace and joy, to live royally and happily in a sacred home that elevates your life, uplifts your spirit, restores your soul, and connects you with the flow of love and prosperity of the universe."

Jagat Singh Khalsa:
FIND YOUR TRUE AUTHENTIC SPACE

Creating a sacred home environment isn't a matter of aesthetics; of throwing money at our homes; of filling them with elegant, stylish, or expensive items according to classical or modern design theories. That's the kind of home Jagat grew up in. Every room was picture-perfect, all of it perfectly designed—for a magazine shoot but not necessarily for living in.

When Jagat was twelve, his house was featured in an upscale magazine. And it looked beautiful in the magazine! It was an artificially elegant environment, designed and set up to photograph well and impress readers. It was picture-perfect; it just wasn't a home he felt completely at home in.

There were rooms in the home that he never went into. To him they felt sterile and uninviting. They were designed aesthetically but without taking him into account. He felt uncomfortable in them, as if he didn't belong. There was no place in them for him just to be. The only places where he felt at home, and where he spent significant time, were his bedroom, the playroom in the basement, and the kitchen. The rest of the house was mostly space he passed either through or by.

Many years later, Jugat had the opportunity to spend time in a wide variety of altared spaces. He visited and worshiped in mosques, churches, *gurdwaras* (Sikh temples), other temples, and powerful nature sites. He also discovered that some of the most powerful altared and sacred spaces were in private homes. And he learned the difference between the beautiful, the elegant, the spectacular, the well designed — and the sacred. An altared space can embody all four qualities mentioned above, but those qualities do not in themselves constitute the sacred, just as the stylish magazine photo shoot of his childhood home was not a visual record of a sacred home but rather a designer's palate.

Take one moment here and think about the different homes you've spent time in, whether of friends, family, or acquaintances. Which one of these homes feels the best, the warmest, the calmest, and the most comfortable, the one where time seems to pass in relaxed enjoyment? Now, is the home you picked the one with the most expensive decor, the home with the most spectacular stuff? I've done this little exercise myself, and the answer was a definitive no! There's something else, something almost intangible and indefinable, in the homes where we feel the most comfortable, peaceful, and at home. Money, artistry, and impressive things do not, in themselves, make a sacred space.

Little Touches to Spruce Up Your Space

But it's not just about identifying what your space needs, it's also about finding out what's *working* in your environment right now and making sure to keep it there. What things do you *like* about your home right now? These can be textures, smells, and beautiful things you have that just make you smile whenever you see them or experience them.

Even though these "touches" might seem like nothing to you, they subtly change the way you feel about yourself and your world. Think about it this way: When you walk into a cold, sterile doctor's office with graphs and charts on the wall, do you feel better? What if the office had warm pictures of smiling people and comfortable places to sit, wouldn't that help you feel more at ease?

Clear the Clutter

Keep the clutter out of your space—and your life. Just as you're supposed to lower your cholesterol in order to keep your blood flowing, you need to eliminate the clutter that's getting in the way of your *groove* flowing into your life. My mom used to have boxes with stuff from the last twenty years all over the garage. When my father died, we told her she had to get out more, but she said she couldn't, because there were too many boxes to go through and clean up. Then one day my son Quinn, her grandson, asked: "What if you got rid of those boxes and spent more time with us?" That was the leverage she needed to get moving and dump all that old baggage.

Here are some tips for getting rid of your clutter:

- *Get rid of clothes you don't absolutely love.* If you haven't worn it or it doesn't fit, donate it to charity. While you might be waiting to lose some extra weight or for the trends to come back, why fill your closet with things that you can't wear and don't immediately LOVE? (And if you do lose that weight, you can treat yourself to some new outfits!)

QUICK TUNEUP:
QUESTIONS TO HELP YOU
CLEAN UP YOUR LIFE
Go to your closet and ask yourself
these four questions:
1. Do I love it?
2. Do I use it?
3. Do I need it?
4. Does it make me feel good?
If you answered "no" to any of these,
then throw the item away!

- *Fix or replace things that are broken.* When you keep things in your space that don't work, you're encouraging your life to reflect that brokenness.
- *Move your furniture.* If it's difficult for you to move around in a room or a hallway, it's time to move your furniture or get rid of extra pieces. You need to be able to flow from one room to the next, just as you want your happiness to.
- *When you buy something, try to get rid of something.* To keep the flow of energy in your home, be sure that you're always letting something go

when you bring something new into your life. It's a great lesson in being thankful for new things as well as for things that once served a purpose in your life. This also allows you to help someone else in need by donating your old clothes to someone who *will* wear them and appreciate them.

Top Rituals for Creating Your Space

One way to ensure more nurturing, mindful spaces is to create rituals for yourself. Every time I travel to a city, I bring back something that represents what I'm looking for in that moment; for a time I wanted more knowledge, so I brought back books. Then it was comfort (pillows) and serenity (candles). This ritual allowed me to constantly reevaluate my space, to make sure what I surrounded myself with still served me.

Here are some other great ideas for implementing "space" rituals:

Devote One Area to the Things You Love

Create a small space, shelf, corner, or even box that contains things you love (such as religious items, pictures, books, or anything else meaningful to you). Whenever you are feeling you need to reconnect with yourself, go to this space to remind yourself who you are and what you love.

Of the objects on or in your personal area, your choices should be items that make you happy and

remind you of your beauty. Consider adding pictures of
people you love or a time you shared that truly reminds
you that you are blessed.

Clear the Air

This should be a space in which you can truly be yourself and be free to be yourself. To make sure of this,
many people will clear the air around the space to purify
it and to make room for only the best of intentions. Some
people like to ring a bell before going into their personal
space, or they light a candle or some incense to remind
them that they are in a special area.

You can also clear the air by airing your wishes to
others in your family and in your group of friends. Talk
to them about your need to have this private space for
yourself so that they can understand when you need
space and distance from them in your everyday life.

Start a Collection

I once knew a woman who saw a picture of a Buddha on a
T-shirt in a store, and before she knew it, she had bought
the shirt and was out the door with it in a bag. She wasn't
necessarily a Buddhist, nor did she want to become a
part of this path, but there was something about the sym-
bol of Buddha—the peace, the serenity— that spoke to
her. Over the years she has accumulated Buddha statues
that sit around her office. This collection allows her to
showcase the peace that she wants for herself, and these

symbols have even become small signposts in her path to success.

Without any backup plan or safety net, she decided to leave her secure job and become a freelance writer. And wouldn't you know it? One of her first writing assignments was about Buddhism—when she was wearing the shirt she bought. She had something that constantly reminded her to be peaceful in every moment—and in the end, she made peace with her dreams.

Try to find something that you can collect, even if it's simply leaves from trees, that speaks to you and reminds you of who you are at your core or who you wish to be.

Surround Yourself with the Sounds of Love
Incorporating as many senses as you can into your personal space is crucial to surrounding your soul with reminders of your value and power in this world. You might want to add a musical background to your life in order to constantly remind yourself of the love you have and that you want in your life. Whether you like classical, jazz, rock, world beat, easy listening, or traditional music of any culture or period, the music that stirs your soul is your sacred music. And you may want to vary the music depending on the occasion. What do you like to listen to when you're cooking in the kitchen? When you're reading or relaxing in the living room or bedroom? When you're winding down before bed, meditating,

waking up in the morning, or preparing for your day? Music is nice to go to bed to and to wake up to. Try a stereo with a sleep timer that turns your music off at night and on again in the morning.

Take Yourself on a Journey of the Senses

I'm a big advocate for creating the full sensory experience for your personal space—that is, combining as many senses as you can: smell, touch, sound, taste, and sight. For one day or for every day, try to find things that will stimulate these senses and make you feel more comfortable in your own space.

Color alone can inspire a variety of different moods. In *Altar Your Space* Jagat outlines how different colors can affect how we feel:

- *Pink*: Physically, mentally, and emotionally soothing. It enlivens compassion, love, and purity.
- *Yellow:* Awakening and mentally activating. It stimulates intellectual activity.
- *Red*: Stimulates the mind and body. It encourages sexuality and passion. It can be extreme and very powerful. Use it wisely and sparingly.
- *Green*: Brings balance, encourages growth, and instills calm.
- *Blue:* Enhances creative expression. It is peaceful and expansive, like the sky.

- *Purple*: Has a hypnotic effect. It encourages intense emotions, from anger to sublimity. It should be used very sparingly.
- *Orange:* Activates optimism and refuels energy reserves.

QUICK TUNEUP
Think about which colors you want to showcase and why. What emotions do you want to feel each day?

Get Out into Nature
Nature is a universal personal space. Since we all live in nature, just different shades of it, going back to the earth and to its simplicity can help us reconnect more deeply with our lives. Try heading to local parks or hiking trails once a week just to remember the stillness of nature and the quiet in your soul.

Top Strategies for Creating Your Space
One of the main reasons we pick up home and garden magazines (at least for me!) is that we're always looking for fun and creative ways to dress up our space that represent who we are and make us feel good. This is why it's called *your* space, because it reflects the best of who *you* are. Discovering these strategies to create *your* space is

crucial, as they help you feel at peace when you're at home or in the office; you want to accept and love the space you're in, and always feel fully present.

Clear the Clutter

You need to make space for your space, but you already knew that, didn't you? In addition, you already know how beneficial it is to clear the physical clutter from your life, but what about the other clutter we all have around us? What about those commitments we keep even though we don't want to keep them? What about those things we say yes to that we really don't want to do? Maybe it's time to clear some clutter from your schedule so that you have time for yourself in your space.

Create an Area to Nurture All the Parts of You

We aren't simple creatures, are we? We don't like just one thing and feel that one thing supports us; we believe that many things support us and help nurture us. It's not only the bubble bath (though that does sound good right now), but it's also the time spent walking around a bookstore. Think about the things that truly fill you up in your soul and then create a space that celebrates them all.

There is a great exercise I learned years ago from my friend, Jayme Barrett:

- Tap your heart a few times and imagine a pink rose inside.

- Visualize people you have in the pink rose; send them love, light, strength, and prosperity.
- Send love around the world.
- Send energy to your family, career, and projects, and see them blooming.
- Give thanks, open your eyes, then move to circulate your energy.
- Write a response to these questions in your journal: What's different about your environment now? How did this quick exercise make you feel?

Give Each Room Its Own Identity

Why limit your space to just one room in your home? Try to bring a piece of yourself to every room in your home so that you feel comfortable and supported no matter where your day takes you. You should also encourage your family to create their own spaces in the house so that they can have a "home base" to turn to as well. Or, you might want to create a "peaceful" room, a "play" room, and other such themes around your home to give you different places to turn to during different moods.

Keep It Light

Remember to see your life through the eyes of a child—with innocence, wonder, and curiosity. You want to create a life that's fun and exuberant, full of energy. To do this, don't believe you always need to be serious. A toy every now and then never hurt anyone. Neither did a humorous quote or a funny movie poster in your personal space.

> *We do not stop playing because we grow old, we grow old because we stop playing!*
> —BENJAMIN FRANKLIN

Plant a Garden

The opportunity to cultivate a garden is an amazing experience. Because you get to choose the plants you want to nourish, as well as the results you want to have, you can think of this garden as your own seeds (your wishes) that grow into flowers (your dreams). Even if you don't have a green thumb, a simple houseplant can be a soul-filling pleasure. Make it a ritual to talk to your plants, tell them to grow and how beautiful and full of life they are (then tell yourself the same!).

Create Your Power Office

If you head to an office every day, like so many of us do, why not introduce your personal space to this area where you spend so much of your life? Bring little things that remind you of happy times or things that remind you of your bigger dreams outside the working world. This will help you come into work excited to be there and help you to be more creative. If you want to bring something new in your life (for example, an intimate relationship), add a touch of romance to the room—maybe fresh roses or a poster featuring your favorite big-screen couple (whether that be Tom and Meg or Ingrid and Bogie).

Create Your Ideal Day

Before you go to a grocery store, you have a list of the things you want to buy, right? Why not do the same before you start your day? For a few minutes in the morning, why not close your eyes and create the ideal day in your head. Visualize what you want to happen between the time you head out the door to the time you go to bed.

One Last Assignment: Review Your Home

Do this fun little review of your home (whether it be an apartment or house) and think about what you have learned about YOU that you could share with your home environment. Bring your journal to capture all that you feel. Notice how you feel when you first walk in. What are you immediately drawn to? Pay attention to colors, senses, and objects. Ask yourself the following questions as you enter each room:

- Does this represent me and how I want to feel?

- What is the feeling I want to experience in this space and do I feel that way?
- What would I need to do to enhance this space without spending a lot of money or time?
- What do I need to let go of in order to have the space I desire?
- How will I feel when my home is a reflection of me?

My hope is that your home becomes that sanctuary we all seek—one that encourages you to be your true self and represent who you are. I know I've thrown a lot at you in these last several chapters—thanks for sticking with it and committing to something greater in your life!

I'm curious: What specific things have you learned about yourself? What actions have you taken as a result of something you read here? What have you learned that you are committed to tuning-up/sharing with other women?

But we're not done yet! I have two more important pieces I would like to share with you . . .

Umuntu Ngumuntu Ngabantu.
  I Am Because We Are.

I learned this Zulu phrase in Africa from my friend Philippe. It means that we are interconnected; we all share a common fate; that your problems are my problems; that what we have in common is much more important than our interesting differences; that we can only really be complete if we care for others at least as much as we care for ourselves.

CHAPTER 8

Make a Commitment to Yourself and Your World

The problem is: We CAN'T stand still—our world needs us too much right now. For this final chapter together, I really want to acknowledge you. It takes a lot of courage to pick up a book like this. A LOT! It's much easier to pick up a magazine and get wrapped up in someone else's life and neglect your own. But it's a rare person who says: *I want to make my life better; I want to make* me *better. I know that there is a lot more of me to bring to the table.* Now is the time to celebrate making it through a good part of this journey and demand something more for yourself.

Here are two final gifts for you:

1. The power of incorporating all that you've learned. Decide to make this book a part of who you are. Embrace the thoughts, feelings, and actions stirred by these pages and make them a ritual for your life so you can embrace all you deserve. Decide to make

taking care of you and nurturing your core a priority so that you can give with even more intention.

2. The magic of contribution and giving back to your world. Once you've made a difference in yourself, then you are empowered to share your gifts and help those around you—your family, friends, and community.

PART ONE:
Integrating the Shifts
You Have Made

Think about how far you've come! We can become so focused on where we are right now, or what's going wrong, and how much further we have to go, that we can forget where we started. Not too long ago, you were thinking that you'd NEVER be where you are right now. And guess what? You are.

Take some time to appreciate this internal growth by thinking about things you used to do but don't anymore. You can even laugh a little at yourself at how you used to be frazzled, while now you're a little calmer in the face of chaos. Or maybe instead of always telling yourself you don't have time to start running, a passion of yours back when, you decided now was the time to rekindle that love. Or maybe you're taking a look around your space, remembering how it used to be a blank uninspiring canvas, and how it now defines your personal style. Sure, you may still be working toward where you want to be, but you are much better off than you were had you never tried to do anything. Even if it is just one tuneup, you never know how that will show up to make your life (or someone else's life) better.

Stay Connected to the Right People and Resources

Now that you've made these shifts in your life, make sure you surround yourself with a team that will support you and hold you accountable to these changes. Ensure that you keep in touch with the things, people, and resources that help you stay true to your core. Just because you're "better" than you were before doesn't mean you don't need to keep helping yourself and others.

I created my company, Lobella, as an opportunity for women of all ages and backgrounds to stay connected, to grow and learn together, to hold each other accountable, and to cheer each other on, especially for those times when they feel as if no one else is supporting them. So come be a part of it. Even though we all live in different places around the world, we can still be there for each other (visit www.lobella.com).

And remember: You are NOT alone. Women in particular seem to shoulder the burdens of their lives alone, even though we don't have to. I understand it, really, I do. I wanted to be the strong, independent mom who could work many hours a day while also growing a healthy and happy child in my womb. I wanted to be the one who never seemed to have any troubles, no matter what life threw at me. But life does happen, and you will have your ups and downs.

The truth for me was, I was tired and I did need help. I just didn't open my mouth and ask for it at first! And I could have made it a lot easier on myself if I had stepped up and asked for help every now and then. And when I finally did—wow!—life was amazing! You don't have to make that mistake; you can join the universal sisterhood of support. You don't have to be the martyr and fight for everything yourself. When challenges arise, we need to rely on our friends and loved ones for help and guidance. And sometimes life gives us a little push to make sure that happens . . .

Doris: A PILGRIMAGE OF LOVE AND SUPPORT

For more than ten years, Doris wanted to hike the Catholic pilgrimage in Spain called the Camino de

Santiago de Compostela. It's a total of 500 miles from the French border to Santiago de Compostela, including climbing several mountain passes as high as 5,000 feet and enduring some extreme weather conditions—you could walk through dry heat one day, snow on the mountaintop on another, or rain for days.

A very proud two-time New York Marathon finisher, Doris accepted the challenge. With little information, a heavy (eighteen pounds!) backpack, some new hiking shoes, and a hiking guide, she traveled to Burgos.

The night before her first day of hiking, she called her mom. She told her mom that she was fearful that she might not be able to complete the hike. She confessed that since she had sold the family business (a small countryside hotel) four years ago, she had felt guilty for selling something grounded in 150 years of history. Two aunts had hardly spoken to her since the sale. So—being a good Catholic girl—Doris hoped that completing the pilgrimage would move God (and her aunts) to forgive her.

On the tenth day of the hike, Doris was bitten by a spider, which introduced a flesh-eating bacteria into her bloodstream. Doctors at a local

Spanish hospital cut her right leg open in order to save it. Despite her life-threatening situation, Doris didn't contact anyone. Because she had always been "Super Doris," she felt she could do anything herself, and she didn't want to be a burden to anyone (have you ever felt that way, and kept quiet because you didn't want your family or friends to worry?).

She underwent two surgeries, and the doctors tried to cut out the infected skin and flesh. Because she wasn't getting any better, she was then airlifted to a hospital in her hometown of Vienna, Austria.

Doctors there opened her bandage and told her she needed emergency surgery that very night or she would lose her leg. It was a risky procedure: Seventy-five percent of people diagnosed with the bacteria die within the first thirty-six hours; 92 percent of the rest have their extremities amputated.

Doris then realized how dire her situation truly was. She texted the one person in her circle of friends who she knew was closest to God: her best friend Gerry, in Ireland. Fearful that she would lose her leg or her life, Doris asked Gerry to pray for her. Then the nurses rolled her into the surgery room.

At seven o'clock the next morning, Doris checked her phone. The display showed 280 new messages; people from all over the world wanted to let her know that they were praying for her and with her in spirit.

A close friend flew in from Chicago to be with Doris; two more came from London, followed by dozens of flowers, chocolates, bears, healing devices, healing stones, and tons of phone calls! The doctors and nurses thought they had a rock star in their care!

After four weeks in the hospital, Doris survived with her leg and foot intact; and her aunts are grateful she's alive and connecting with her once again. Now Doris knows miracles do happen and that we must reach out to our friends, family, God, and community for help, in any situation.

The bottom line: We can't wait until a life-threatening situation comes along to allow others to take care of us! Doris and the other amazing women in this book are sharing their stories in the hopes that they will help. They also want to let every woman out there know: No one is alone here. Help is always close by, ready to jump in at a moment's notice.

Nurture Your Support System

One of our greatest resources is the network of girlfriends we create, nurture, and cherish throughout our lifetime. (If you don't have a strong group just yet, think about who you can engage! It may be the neighbor you were too shy to talk to, or a colleague from work you always admired. Now's the time to create your network of support!) Think about all of the amazing women who have come in and out of your life. What have you learned from your friendships with these women? What can you do to cultivate these relationships? How can you together share the joys, sorrows, fears, and triumphs of each of your lives?

Make a list of your closest friends (maybe there are fabulous people in your life that you have lost touch with and you want to bring them back into your life); get their phone numbers, e-mail addresses, and birthdays; and make a concerted effort to stay in touch with these women regularly—whether that's once a week or once a month.

Here's what I do. (Once again I make it a necessity, because we always seem to connect at "just the right time.")

- I always call my friends on their birthdays or send a card. Yes, I send an actual card, one that reminds me of them in some unique way. At the beginning of the year, I make a sheet with everyone's name on it, go to the card store, and buy my cards for the year. When I get home, I address and stamp them all, then sort them by the months. At the beginning of each month, I take an hour to personalize them and off they go!!

- I schedule at least one day a month to make sure I do something with one of my friends, such as go see a movie, get our nails done, or have tea.
- I keep my friends "present" in my life through pictures in my house and in my planner.
- I keep a list of nifty fifty: These are the top fifty men and women whom I would do anything for. I program their names in my phone under my favorites, assign them each a special ringtone, and set my alarm on my phone to "schedule" my time of when I will call them to check in at least once a week. (An example of a ringtone: For my best friends I use "Lean on Me.")
- I also have created info sheets on some of my friends that include their favorite colors, flowers, books, collectibles, and so on.
- I have become friends with a few women who are much older than me. Because I know we share so much in common, I make sure we do lunch at least once a month.

You will probably have certain friends with whom you connect often, and others whom you may only speak to a few times a year. It is important to cherish these different friends for what they bring to your life, and let them know once in a while why they are so important to you. Often keeping up with our friends is the first thing to go when we're stressed out and overwhelmed, yet it is one of those areas that brings us balance and joy during the toughest of times.

> *Each friend represents a world in us, a world possibly not born until they arrive, and it is only by this meeting that a new world is born.*
> —ANAÏS NIN

Friends are the people whom you can turn to when your world is turning upside down (think back to Doris's story—we can't be afraid to turn to one of our greatest resources). They are a network of people with whom you share your ideas, your dreams, and maybe even your tears. Defining who is and who is not a friend is not the most important thing—bringing them into your life is.

My life is so rich with many textures of women. When I look at all of my friends, I see the biggest tapestry. Okay, maybe it's more like a patchwork quilt!

The one thing I do know for sure is that when one of my friends needs me, I commit to being there for her and, sometimes, I just need to trust that the other "things" will get done.

Joelle: THE POWER OF SISTERHOOD

"I'm sorry, ma'am, there's been an accident—we did everything we could." Joelle would never forget the knock at her door at almost four o'clock in the morning on November 29, 2001. The loss of her husband, Eric, felt like a blow to her chest.

Within hours, we all arrived (her closest friends from all over the country) at her home and never left; many of us stayed for weeks. We were like butterflies swirling around as we took over the day-to-day operations of her life. The phone calls were answered, the food was made, Joelle's son was adored, the house was cleaned, the funeral arrangements made; we even picked out something for her to wear the day of the funeral.

They say you can never be prepared for a tragedy to strike, but after this experience and others since, Joelle believes we can be emotionally and spiritually prepared. We can be prepared by choosing to live a powerful life every day. We can choose to find the joy, the peace, the meaning, and the love to make each day worthwhile. We can choose to make a difference in the world. We can find humor in even the most devastating situations. And we can choose to live big and love big.

The other way we can be prepared is to surround ourselves with extraordinary people. Joelle never could have made it through with her son without an army of incredible loving people who were there for them every day—not just in the beginning but for the long haul.

For us, it wasn't just about saying we would be there for Joelle—we all made a commitment and stuck to it. We have to continue to show up for each other. It's like going to the gym—one session on the treadmill is not going to give you the body you've always dreamed of! You need to keep nurturing your relationships and make sure you cherish your friends and give them your full support.

When you gotta go and be there for your girlfriends—go, and go now! You never know how you can make a difference.

Use Role Models and Mentors to Hold Yourself Accountable

Within this network you will gather together women who inspire, challenge, and remind you of all that is possible. Your time together will not always be easy. If you remember from the very beginning of this book, I had a friend who was willing to be unpopular with me, and tell me things I maybe didn't want to hear, to help me grow. Most of my role models are those every day heroes, those women and men in the trenches—women like YOU. Look around, these women are everywhere.

You need to continue to create the energy of positive feelings and positive results. This will not only inspire you, it will also ensure that you have someone to help guide you when you're feeling a bit lost.

You can also have role models and mentors who you do not actually know or meet. Personally, I love to read the biographies of great women in history or read about women in the news who are helping the world to be a better place. I always ask: What can I learn from these women, and how can I model some of the qualities that they exemplify? When you take the time to learn more about other women, you begin to determine how you can change your life in order to be more like them in those areas you admire. Do you think of Madonna or Angelina Jolie as role models because of all of their humanitarian work? Or do you admire Christina Applegate, strong and determined in her own fight against breast cancer, because of her efforts to raise money to find a cure? Well, you can emulate that side of them in your own life by finding ways to contribute in your own community.

By surrounding yourself with women you respect and making sure to learn from them, you can become the woman you most admire. For example, take a moment to look around the room you're in. Take special care to notice only the blue things in the room. Keep a mental picture in your head of these objects, as well as a list of what they are. Now, close your eyes and try to list all of the red things in the room. Hard to do, isn't it?

What happens with this exercise is that you focus on only one thing, which makes other things in the room seemingly disappear—even though they are there all along. By surrounding yourself with mentors and role models, and even just reading about positive women in the world, you begin to notice positive attributes in yourself and in your world. What's even better is that you are often drawn to people who are similar to you. So that woman that you admire so much? She's just another version of you—but *she's* the one that you're taking notice of. Time to shift your focus and take notice of yourself.

Envision Your Future

I'm sure I've used this analogy before, but it really rings true for me: When you go on a trip to a foreign place, you need a map. But you also need a vision in your head of what this place is going to be like. Why would you have taken off on the trip in the first place? You don't go somewhere (unless you're more adventurous than me) without having some clue as to what you want the location to be like.

With all the self-work you have done with this book, you need to make sure you take some time to envision who you will be—a strong, powerful, and magnificent woman. But just as any other trip, you also want to enjoy the "ride." Take some time to look out the windows of your journey. Appreciate the steps you take; appreciate the process. Life is a journey, not a destination, after all. This is going to be a process that continues on throughout your life, which means you need to pace yourself.

Three Final Steps to Stay True to Your Core

It's often the simpler lessons in life that are the most difficult to remember, particularly when life feels a bit overwhelming. There are three mantras I constantly remind myself of, particularly when I've been going nonstop. I know that if I remember these truths, I will stay true to who I am, despite what else is going on in the world.

Check in with Yourself

Think about your car. If the engine light comes on, and you just keep on driving, you may be ignoring the fact that something is not working the way it should be. Similarly, you need to be sensitive to the different signals your body and mind send to you. And this doesn't just mean constantly moving. Sometimes we mistake activity with progress. But action doesn't necessarily mean progress. Progress means making decisions that change you for the better, with your best interest in mind.

Checking in with how you feel is the best way to know when you're not being authentic. When you do or say something that is not who you really are, you feel a heaviness in your heart. When this happens, the important thing is to catch yourself quickly. Ask yourself some questions to change your focus: Who am I really doing this for? What is my real outcome here? What is the most important thing in this interaction?

Remember, too, the larger contexts of the tougher moments. Sometimes you have to walk through a difficult situation to get to what really matters. Sometimes it's important to appreciate the tougher moments, too, and just let them be so that what's next and better for you has the space to grow.

Take Care of the Foundation First

We've talked about this before—you cannot live your truth if you are feeling tired, stressed, resentful, or frustrated. Only when you have a strong physical and emotional base will you have the energy to let your real intent come through. When you want to buy a house, who do you send out first? The home inspector. And if he says the foundation is weak, does he tell you to buy the house? No way! So you need to nurture the important things in your life that build your foundation: your health, relationships, finances, contribution, and so on. Otherwise your house is built on sand (and not a foundation of love, passion, fulfillment, and joy.)

Let Your Life Flow

At its core, authenticity is about flow, not push. Life unfolds for you when you let go and let things happen, not when you plan how every moment is supposed to be. Being authentic should not be an effort. A fire hose works when there is a smooth, continuous path for water to flow through; but sometimes a kink stops that water. Don't be the stop gap for your own progress and happiness.

Imagine moments in your life when you are totally happy, free, and at peace. Are you at a concert just taking in the music, dancing for no reason at all? Are you with your kids? Are you enjoying an evening with your spouse? Are you laughing with your friends? These are the moments when your authentic self comes out—when you understand that being real isn't just about you, it's about appreciating and enjoying the beauty of what's around you.

Strive to appreciate these moments and let life in. When you are always planning and pushing for things to happen, you miss out on all the elements that make you whole.

The human contribution is the essential ingredient. It is only in the giving of oneself to others that we truly live.

—ETHEL PERCY ANDRUS

PART TWO:
The Gift of Contribution

Nothing in life is permanent. Life changes, we change, we grow. One thing for sure is that we have many choices in our lives. But we must learn to choose wisely. Every day we make decisions about who we want to hang around with, what we need to focus on, what we choose to do, and who we choose to be. It is easy to get distracted with all of the choices available to us. In the end, we all truly want to make a difference; we want to leave the world a little better than when we came. Now that we have improved our lives, we need to, as my friend Michael Hutchinson says, "clean up our own backyard." It's time for a Women's Revolution, and we need to lead the charge to help support each other. Not just your girl-friends or family, but every woman!

The challenge for many of us is that we want to take action, but we fear we have nothing to offer. When we fear we have nothing to offer, how can we give anything? We each have gifts to share, and it's selfish not to share those gifts! (If you're still wondering what those gifts are, go back to your journal and take a look at the passions that make you unique—these are your gifts that must be shared with the world!)

With those gifts comes our duty to take care of and give back to the community around us. Our gifts are like a fantastic secret that no one else can share—if you are my friend and you know something that will make my life better, wouldn't you want me to know it?

Think about when you plant bulbs in a garden in the fall. You can't see what they're going to do when it is cold and snowing outside, but come spring, they poke their little flowers out from underneath the soil and begin to transform into something beautiful. But here is the truth: They have to planted so that they can and will grow, which means you have to take your gifts and put them to work! I know it is not always easy, but it is a decision you have to make. Schedule a time to do it and trust that all of that hard work will pay off! Here's the thing: You have NO idea how many people will benefit from the beauty of your garden. And you'll never know until you put your shovel to soil.

Moving from Ideology to Action

While realizing you have something to offer is a great start, it doesn't mean anything unless you start taking ACTION. Here are some simple ways to find out how you can help others:

- *Think about the things you like to do.* If you like kids, then help organizations that help kids. If you love connecting with other people and hearing personal stories and experiences, then volunteer at a nursing home. Whatever your passion, you can find an opportunity to fill it.

- *Look for opportunities to make someone's day just a little better.* Contribution is not just about money; it's about giving back any part of you— including your time and effort. This can be as simple as helping someone with groceries, opening a door for someone, or giving someone a smile next time you're crammed in the elevator after a long day at work.

- *Realize that you don't always know when you're going to change someone's day, or life, around.* A participant at one of my events shared a story about how he, working as a waiter, had seen a lady crying in the back of the restaurant. He walked over and asked her if she wanted "the best chowder in Newport Beach." She resisted at first, then allowed him to bring her chowder and sit down next to her. Later he found out that she was crying because she had just lost her eighteen-month-old and was thinking about taking her own life. One small random act of kindness had changed this woman's fate completely. You never know who or how you can help—don't miss out on a great opportunity to make an impact.

- *Be an example of doing what's right.* From bringing your own bags to the grocery store to letting the car in front of you have the right of way, be a role model of taking care of your world and the people in it. My husband, Shore, was walking down a street as a young boy when his father gave him a piece of gum. Shore threw the wrapper on the ground; his dad quietly picked it up and put it in his pocket. Though his dad never said a word, this little experience had a profound effect on Shore. He could never litter after that, and in that moment he realized the power of being an example. He passed that lesson on to his own children, and we noticed the processional effect with our son, Quinn, who was skiing when he saw a water bottle dropped on the slope—he grabbed it and put in his jacket to throw away later.

- *Think international.* Your efforts don't have to be limited to your own country. Is there a cause you're passionate about that affects another country or region? You *can* make an impact, even another world away. I speak from experience—I have traveled to many places around the world, yet I felt very compelled to go to Malawi. I have a lot of friends who said they would like to go but "had to wait" until their kids were out of school in a few years. When I heard that, I thought: *A few years? A few years may be too late!* I thought about how many times I had said, "I'll do it later," and then never did it. I decided I had to go there NOW so that I could share about all the children I had met and tell my kids how we could all make a difference NOW.

RAISING MALAWI ACADEMY FOR GIRLS: TRANSFORMATION THROUGH EDUCATION

Mercy is a thirteen-year-old girl in Malawi. Remember when you were thirteen? Mercy is the oldest member of her household. Every day she cooks only one meal for her five siblings, gathers the firewood, and collects water from an unprotected well about two miles from her small, one-room hut. She can't afford to attend school. She can't afford to eat every day. She can't afford the eighty-cent medicine that could protect her, her brothers, and her sisters from malaria. Her father, before he died of an AIDS-related disease, often beat her and her siblings mercilessly. He never earned more than fifty cents a day. Now Mercy (an orphaned child) is the leader of her family.

Mercy is one of countless girls in sub-Saharan Africa who deal with the effects of HIV/AIDS, poverty, and disease. Sadly, she has been reduced to a statistic.

But there is a solution.

The brightest minds from the leading research organizations have done the math: When you disempower young women, serious problems occur that can bring a country to its knees—economics suffer, mortality rates rise, disease erupts. But if we invest in girls' education and their overall well-being, we can literally transform nations. We can transform the world.

Founded on the spirit of Umunthu (Chichewa for "I am because we are"), the Raising Malawi Academy for Girls is dedicated to inspiring within each student a sense of global and individual responsibility. Directed by my friend Phillippe van den Bossche, the Academy is important to me, because if we can help girls in one of the poorest countries feel a sense of pride about who they are, imagine what we can do in our own backyards! We don't have five or ten years to do this. We have to start now.

This is a cause that is very dear to my heart. I've had some people ask me how I could be focused on something so far away when there are so many needy causes here at home. My answer to that: How can I not? I got involved because I had been all over the world and needed to contribute to something that could really use my help. At a Madonna concert a few years ago, a statistic came on the screen: *By the year 2012, 21 million children will be orphaned because of AIDS.* That's when I realized: I have to go to Malawi.

I'd like to invite you to join me and women around the world as we make a difference for the Raising Malawi Academy for Girls. There are three ways to get involved domestically: Do research, be a part of the awareness team, or do fund-raising. For more information please visit www.raisingmalawi.org.

Giving Back:
A Tool to Stay True to Your Core

I think sometimes it's easy to overlook one huge benefit of giving back: what it does to help you stay true to who you are.

I learned so many unexpected lessons when I ran my first marathon a few months ago. First, I had to sign up and commit. Second, I needed to run for something bigger than myself. I realized the reason I personally had never committed to doing a marathon was that I didn't want to make it about me. So I decided to join Team in Training for the Leukemia and Lymphoma Society.

I committed to raising money and trainings, and I met some amazing people I never would have met. I set aside two hours every Saturday for me to do the long workouts. I prepared, and I did everything they told me to do to have a successful experience with the marathon. I threw out everything I thought I knew and just listened. And when I shut up and just did what they said, I loved the discovery of NOT knowing all the answers. I was a kid again.

Then the big day came: the Alaska Marathon. This wasn't your typical marathon—it was filled with trails, gravel, and hills. But I also noticed at the beginning of the marathon that there were lots of people there to cheer us all on. I decided before the race that I would write the names of my friends and family on my arm. Each time I ran a mile, I would think about that person and what I loved about them. When I got to about mile eight, I noticed that I was spending most of the time by myself; at mile fourteen I was running for my son Jos and tripped on a rock. They call that a "wake-up call."

I got to the mile-fifteen first aid station, and they bandaged me up. I hurt, I was in pain, I didn't know if I could go on. The first aid tech said I should stop— but I knew I needed to keep going. I could hear my grandmother's voice in my head, questioning me when I wanted to do a walkathon as a young girl ("How are you going to do that—you're only ten!"). Inside of me I knew

I had to take one step at a time. Just like life—you just need to take one step at a time.

At the end of the race, once again there were lots of people cheering me on, but those miles of pain and discovery were what made me remember who I was. I remembered what I had to tune into to stay true to myself At the end of the race, with my knee throbbing, I became the woman I most admire—all because I decided to give back to my world.

Who knows what you may find out about yourself when you start on your journey of contribution. It's not about the finish line, it's about being present and learning more about who you really are.

Thank you for the opportunity to share my passion, my stories, and my exercises with you. I hope that these little tuneups got you to wake up to your gifts and to decide that now is the time to live your truth. Even though we may never meet, I hope that you know that I do not take this lightly. I know you had to commit your time away from something else in order to read this book, and I hope you will pass it on to another amazing woman so that she too can discover her passions and remember it is time to share her gifts.

I encourage you to not just put this book back on the shelf—please, don't put *you* back on the shelf! The world needs you now. Commit to moving forward and continuing to grow. The journey doesn't end here. Go tune in to *your* station, and may you always remember the amazing woman you are and stay true to who you are.

Acknowledgments

I must acknowledge all the people who have helped me live and practice what I am here to share with the world. Each has shown me that the real gift is a life that *works* and therefore leaves us feeling deeply fulfilled *every day*. This book has taken shape because it is real life. We've heard people say, "Life would be so easy if it weren't for the people." But it's really the people who make life rich. These people have given my life so much texture and are the reason this book has taken form.

FAMILY

My dad, who is still one of my greatest teachers. His dedication to a life of service in helping others has always inspired me to do the same. Even though he is not in the physical world anymore, I hear his voice and his guidance every day by watching him live through my children.

My mom, who embraces life fully. Her courage and faith inspire all. And that laugh!

My husband Shore, for always being there to help me to do my life's work, as I am always here to help him to do his life's work.

My son, Josua, for his creativity and ability to make me laugh when I need it the most. (I am actually looking forward to his teenage years.) My son, Quinn, for his deep caring for everyone and everything.

Acknowledgments

My daughter, Asher, for adding the girlie sweetness to my life and reminding me that we are all perfect just the way we are.

My brother, David, for his heart; and his wife, Heidi, and his daughter, Lila.

The rest of my family: aunts, uncles, cousins, in-laws, nieces, and nephews.

FRIENDS

Lara Asher, for giving form to my passion and for believing that what I do helps so many people.

Gina Onativia, for jumping in at the last minute, for her late-night brainstorms with me, and her flexibility.

Brittney Hanson, for always capturing "the shot" and for her friendship.

Heidi Krupp Lisiten, for being my fan and letting the world know at every turn what I am doing. D, you got a good one!

My friends and their families. They are the ones who love me, challenge me, and let me "test" my ideas on them—even the crazy ideas that they just roll their eyes at and say to themselves, *Here she goes again.* God Bless 'em! Joelle, Tani, Jayne, Tina, Emily, Adam, Monty, Chris D., Michelle C., Monique W., Wendy D., Ann and Sam S., Anne T., Becky, Julie B., Alissa, Jenn S., Vanessa H., Jill B., Rachael K., Dallyce and Scott, Sissy M., Wendy L., Joanne G., Alison, Jan, and the list goes on and on!

Acknowledgments

Everyone I have had the honor to personally coach one on one past, present, and future.

My constant companions on the road: Mary, Pauline, Robyn, Brandy, Brenda, Pam, Talonya, Margaret, Muni, Pam, Joseph, Marshonda, Gary, Sam, Stan, John, and many more! All the RRI Crew and Trainers I have worked hand in hand with over the past twenty years.

My Life Mastery Support team over the past eight years and every Life Mastery participant I have had the privilege to work with.

For Tony and Sage Robbins, for twenty years of love and support.

All the Lobella Ladies and future Lobella Attendees and Life Tuneups Attendees: for your commitment to Stay True to Who You Are and Your Desire to share your gifts with the world especially: Dayna, Heather, Stephanie, Amanda, Courtney, Dipti, Kate, Taylor, Melody, Amber, Liel, Danielle, Tanya, Marcella and the hundreds of other fabulous women!

NSA and My YOLO Team, for each of your commitments to help make this world a healthier place. Jay Martin, Elton Debois, Danny, Jeff, Cheryl, Missy, Peggy, my team, and the thousands of others.

My home team: Maja, for keeping us organized and being part of our family. Karen for taking such good care of our kids.

Acknowledgments

MENTORS

Many of them I have already mentioned above.

The everyday heroes, women and men who are out there doing good in the world.

All of those involved in the thousands of not-for-profit organizations throughout the world. Your work is love in action.

The Raising Malawi Team, for your commitment to help those who do not have a voice. I have learned so much about true selfless service through all that you do.

Phillipe, you are my mentor, my friend, and my inspiration.

Princess Diana, Mother Teresa, Marianne Williamson, Ellen DeGeneres, Oprah, Angelina Jolie, Madonna, Faith Hill, Bob Proctor, Tony Robbins, Deepak Chopra, Kathy Buckley, James Taylor, Sheryl Crow, Melinda and Bill Gates, Jean Chatzky, Connie Gutterson, Mary Manin Morrissey, Pablo Coelho, Gandhi, and Rosa Parks.

The thing that I am most grateful for is that I choose to have every one of them in my life. They all make my life rich and meaningful. All of these people are my teachers.

About the Author

Loren Slocum is a distinguished international personal development seminar leader, speaker, coach, author, philanthropist, entrepreneur, wife, and mother. People best describe Loren as "the real deal." She has had the remarkable experience of traveling the world to help people discover who they are at their core for the past twenty years.

As crew director for nearly two decades for the recognized authority on the psychology of leadership and peak performance, Anthony Robbins, Loren led and supervised a staff of up to 350 people in cities around the world for events ranging from 1,000 to 20,000 participants.

For the past eight years, Loren has facilitated more than 120 six-day comprehensive programs for Anthony Robbins in the United States, Fiji, Puerto Rico, and Europe that emphasize the power of living in balance. In this program, featuring such influencers as Caroline Myss and Deepak Chopra, Loren has guided people to completely balance themselves—in everything from finances to health, spirituality, and relationships.

Loren is the founder, chief executive officer, and president of Lobella International, an organization inspired to help women "stay true to who they are." She is committed to helping women realize their natural gifts. She is also the author of *No Greater Love: Being an Extraordinary Mom* (1999), which was re-released in April 2008 as *The Greatest Love* and is being sold at Target and Mimi Maternity. Loren has a radio show, Life Tune-ups, on Voice America.

Loren is married to Shore Slocum, also an international speaker, consultant, and entrepreneur, and they have three children: Josua, Quinn, and Asher. Loren is an active volunteer with her children's school and local charities. She is also an active volunteer with Raising Malawi. She is a certified nutritional therapist and teaches health events with her eldest son, Josua, at local schools and groups. She also does keynote speeches and multi-day trainings for many companies around the world. She lives in Henderson, Nevada.